connect

jena forehand

connect

LIVING IN RELATIONSHIPS

NAVPRESS

Discipleship Inside Out

NAVPRESS

Discipleship Inside Out®

NavPress is the publishing ministry of The Navigators, an international Christian organization and leader in personal spiritual development. NavPress is committed to helping people grow spiritually and enjoy lives of meaning and hope through personal and group resources that are biblically rooted, culturally relevant, and highly practical.

For a free catalog go to www.NavPress.com
or call 1.800.366.7788 in the United States or 1.800.839.4769 in Canada.

© 2013 by Jena Forehand

ISBN-13: 978-1-61291-465-7

Cover design by Lux Creative

Some of the anecdotal illustrations in this book are true to life and are included with the permission of the persons involved. All other illustrations are composites of real situations, and any resemblance to people living or dead is coincidental.

Unless otherwise identified, all Scripture quotations in this publication are taken from the *Holy Bible, New International Version®* (NIV®). Copyright © 1973, 1978, 1984 by Biblica, used by permission of Zondervan. All rights reserved. Other versions used include: the *Holy Bible*, New Living Translation (NLT), copyright © 1996, 2004. Used by permission of Tyndale House Publishers, Inc., Wheaton, Illinois 60189. All rights reserved; the New King James Version (NKJV). Copyright © 1982 by Thomas Nelson, Inc. Used by permission. All rights reserved; and *THE MESSAGE* (MSG). Copyright © 1993, 1994, 1995, 1996, 2000, 2001, 2002. Used by permission of NavPress Publishing Group.

Printed in the United States of America

1 2 3 4 5 6 7 8 / 18 17 16 15 14 13

contents

why the LIVING DEEPER series?

I believe that deep within the heart of every woman is a desire to be part of something much bigger than herself. It's an irresistible pull to lock arms with a group of people who share a common passion that transcends the mundane rhythm of each day. This longing calls us to be part of a bigger story that involves risk and ruthless trust, because we know without God's help we are toast.

The great news is that God offers all of us these great adventures to live! The sad news is that most of us choose not to. Fear, inadequacies, insecurities, and doubt (among other things) keep us from ever experiencing life to its fullness.

In the psalms, King David penned, "Deep calls to deep" (Psalm 42:7). In song, he was expressing that the depths of God's heart continually call to the depths of ours.

God wants us to live in deeper relationship with Him. He wants to take us into the deep places where we can know Him fully, follow Him completely, obey Him willingly, and experience Him abundantly. That is what Jesus offers us: "I have come that they may have life, and that they may have it more abundantly" (John 10:10, NKJV).

God is ready to take us by the hand and lead us into the deeper waters of relationship with Him. He wants us to experience the exciting life He created us to live. Aren't you ready to start living deeper?

Join me and thousands of other women who are taking the plunge and heading into the deeper waters with Jesus through this guide. As we move one step at a time, we will be guided to fulfill the very purposes for which we were made. We will also be fulfilling the co-mission offered to us by Christ Himself to join Him: Go and take others with you into the deep. Go and make disciples (see Matthew 28:19). It was His mission and now it is ours. It's time we started really living—living deeper.

How to Use This Guide

The intent of the LIVING DEEPER series is to help women disciple others in an effective way that meets women where they are and takes them into a deeper intimacy with the Father so that they, in turn, can go and make disciples as well. We've coined the phrase, "Be a disciple. Make a disciple. Join the revolution!"

It is the Father's desire that we follow Him as a disciple but also that we make more disciples as we go about our lives. Women all across this country are joining the team to revolutionize this world through the making of disciples, and we are thrilled that you have joined us.

Based on intensive study of how the next generation grows and learns, this book will serve as an experiential guide, combining a variety of means to help the disciple rediscover God's truths on her own through the many different mediums that she both enjoys and thrives on. It is designed to be used as a one-on-one discipleship resource or a small-group resource, keeping in mind that leading a small group also necessitates some one-on-one interaction. Though this guide provides helpful pathways and tools, it allows much flexibility, understanding that each woman leads differently and each disciple learns at her own pace. You have the freedom to follow it precisely or adapt it to the needs of the disciple or group of disciples. Ask the Holy Spirit to show you how to lead each individual, and let Him customize it specifically for her. The main goal is to faithfully disciple others in rediscovering the truth and its implications, while helping them engage God in a deeper, life-altering, and eternally transformational way.

This experiential guide is just that: a conglomeration of experiences to guide followers of Christ into applicable truth. It is broken down into weekly themes, daily nuggets that support the theme, and daily experiences that promote thought, emotion, and intent. Throughout the week, specific exercises will keep the disciple focused and meditating on the truth for that particular week.

Jesus said, "Seek and you will find" (Luke 11:9). So, as you go throughout the week, you will have daily opportunities to Seek Upwardly (What do You want me to learn, Lord? How can I apply this to my relationship with You?), Seek Inwardly (What do You want to change in my heart, Lord? How can I begin to develop this truth in my heart and life?), and Seek Outwardly (What do You want to change in my life so that I can live this truth, taking it out into the world and influencing those around me? What will I do with what You have taught me, Lord?). With each passing day, you will be growing in your relationship with God and your relationship with the others in your group (if you are in one).

As you seek, you will find, and as you find, you will realize you are living in a deeper relationship with God and living out His love on the earth. There is no greater joy than living deeper. So what are you waiting for? Jump in!

a note from the author

Let's face it: Relationships can be so exhilarating, but they can also be gut-wrenching. They can be filled with passion but also filled with pain. Relationships are risky, but those who dare to go there find a richness that others may never attempt. We may have seen glimpses of the good side of relationships, but most of us have experienced to a greater degree the hurtful side. This has caused many of us to steer clear of any kind of depth in our relationships. We're too afraid that deep, penetrating wounds are inevitable. I know this has been true of me.

Why would anyone in their right mind journey into something with proven potential to wound us so deeply? Isn't it just best to isolate ourselves, to protect ourselves from the probability of pain? And without even knowing it, have we projected that same potential for pain onto our relationship with our Creator? Are we keeping Him at arm's length because that is how we have learned to treat others?

The truth is that we were made for a relationship with God and with others, but an adversary has sought to sabotage and twist our perspective of both. We long to know and be known. We long to be intimately understood, with all our flaws, and still be authentically and genuinely loved. That longing is deep . . . really deep within us.

So what do we do with this dichotomy—this desire for deep relationship paired with a deep fear of being wounded—forged deep within our hearts? What do we do when our relationships become so tainted and twisted by this fallen world in which we live?

As I am writing this, my husband has just come in from a run. He untied his well-knotted running shoes and showed me a painful blister that developed during his trek, claiming it was time to get a new pair of shoes. I believe God wants us to untie the proverbial knots we have made in our perspective of relationships. I believe He wants us to examine our current understanding of relationships and remove the misguided perceptions that have caused us pain in the past. I believe He wants us to replace them with the truths that can allow fulfilling, life-giving, and enriching relationships to flourish in our lives.

As we begin this journey together, take a piece of paper and draw a line down the middle to separate it into two columns. In the first column, draw your view of your current relationships or your view of relationships in general. In the second column, draw what you would like to see change in your relationships by the time this eight-week journey is completed. How do you want your relationships to be?

Enjoy your time as you begin living out what relationships are all about!

introduction

We live in a society that is obsessed with relationships and intimacy, but we seem increasingly inept at understanding how to develop them. I believe this inability exists because many people have not experienced a deep and intimate friendship with the original Author of friendship, God. Many don't know the purpose of friendship, the various levels of friendship, and the privileges and responsibilites that accompany each. This is what I hope you will discover as you go through this study.

We were created from intimacy, for intimacy. God is love (see 1 John 4:7-16). It was out of His love that He created us. Because He is the Author of love, He has much love to give us and share with us. His love is perfect love, and He wants to saturate us with it.

God is a relational God. He created us in His image (see Genesis 1:27). Therefore, we are relational creatures and were created for relationships, first and foremost a relationship with Him. He created us for Himself (see Isaiah 43:1). He wants us to enjoy His presence (see Psalm 16:11). He also created us with the desire to be delighted in and enjoyed. God gave us this desire so that we would walk with Him, the very One who knows us better than we know ourselves, and so that He could tell us who He made us to be. Who better to direct our lives than the One who designed us in the first place? Because we were created in His image and we desire to be told who we are, we can deduce that God also loves to be told who He is. We do this when we praise, honor, and worship Him.

Here is the problem: We have chosen to look to others to tell us who we are, neglecting our worship and walk with God, the only One who could really tell us the truth about who we are because He made us! As a result, we have been disappointed, misguided, misidentified, neglected, rejected, and wounded by what others have said about us in both word and action.

You were created for the sole purpose of walking with God. He wants to be delighted in, and He wants to delight in you. What, then, is the end result, or goal, as you walk with God? Becoming holy. Ephesians 1:4 says that before the creation of the world, God created you to be holy. Holy simply means to be "set apart" as completely or wholly His.[1] When God makes you holy (and it's something only God can do), He is restoring you to the way He originally designed you before sin entered the world. When we ask Jesus Christ to be our Savior and Lord, we become wholly His and can then begin our walk with Him. As we walk with Him and He tells us who we are, our lifestyle and actions will begin to reflect that we are wholly His. Hebrews 10:14 says we are holy in our *position* before God (through Jesus, we stand before God not guilty and completely pure because of Jesus' payment for our sin), but are in the *process* of being made holy in our daily practice as we walk with God and let Him help us. God's desire is for our behavior to mirror how He sees us.

Before I met my husband, Dale, I called, hung out with, and dated other guys. My decisions and actions did not affect Dale in any way. But once I took on Dale's name when we married, I became his, completely his. I no longer called other guys or spent time with them or dated them. That commitment to him changed how I related to others. I was completely Dale Forehand's, and he was all mine. My actions influenced and directly affected him. This is what it means

---

1. BlueLetterBible.com.

to be holy. No longer do I spend time with people and things that distract me from walking with God. I took on His name, Christian (which means "little Christ"), and I am all His. Because of this, I need to align my lifestyle and choices with that new name. As I walk with God, He will help me do just that.

How awesome to think that the God of this universe wants to be our friend. He wants us to walk with Him and calls us wholly His. He then helps us become holy in the way we live and gives us just the right friends to help us get there. (If you have never personally asked God to be your friend and would like to know how to do that, please turn to the appendix in the back of this book so you can experience the greatest relationship ever offered you.)

Think about this: If God's desire for you to is to become holy, wouldn't He place just the right people in your life to help you become what He desires for you to become? You see, one of God's main purposes for friendship is to help each other become holy — more wholly and completely devoted to God.

Based on what we have discussed, let's define some very important words before we go any further. For the purposes of this book, a *Christian* is defined as "a friend of God who walks with God and is wholly God's." The *local church* is defined as "a community of friends of God who are all walking with God and striving to be holy in the way they live." Thus, a *Christian friend* is "a fellow friend of God who helps you become more and more holy as you both walk together with God."

How do these new definitions and new purposes for your relationship with God and others change your perspective of relationships? Write down your thoughts in your journal.

I hope you are excited about what lies ahead! Each week you will have five days of study. On day 1 we will discuss a specific aspect of friendship that is necessary for the relationship to progress. Day 2 offers dangers that can cause damage to the friendship. Day 3 looks at an attitude of the heart that we need to ask God to develop in us so that we can have healthy relationships. Day 4 discusses areas to avoid in order to develop healthy relationships. And day 5 offers a commitment that you might want to make to others because Jesus already made it for you! This journey you are taking with God is going to bring a freshness to your relationships. It will also encourage a depth that you may not have experienced in a long time, if ever. I am so thrilled about the transformation that is going to take place. If you are meeting with a small group, don't forget to grab this study, your Bible, and your journal so that you can share and grow with others as you meet. Be open to whatever God wants to teach you on this new journey, and have fun!

the stadium (part 1)

Day 1: Attraction

As you begin today's study, quiet your soul to spend some time with God. Talk with Him about where you are in your current friendships and then make this request: *Holy Spirit, be my Teacher. Give me understanding on how to put what I learn today into practice. In the name of Jesus I ask, amen.* You will be encouraged to pray in this way every single day of this journey. Spiritual things are spiritually discerned, and it is God's Spirit within you that helps you fully understand. To acknowledge your need for God's help includes Him in the process of expanding your view of who He is. You will begin to see His work in your life and begin to live in deeper relationship with Him. When you ask in Jesus' name, you are asking as if Jesus Himself were asking. Your prayer aligns with His desires for you, so you can bet this prayer will be answered!

• • • • • • • • •

Not too long ago, I got sucked into the vacuum of a video game that my son dared me to play with him. I started at the basic level only to find that once I made it through a series of obstacles, there were more challenging levels ahead. Though difficult and frustrating at times, it was also exhilarating and fun when I achieved the goals of one level

17

and was able to move to the next. Our relationships are much the same. There are different levels of relationship, each carrying its own set of privileges, responsibilities, and challenges. For the next eight weeks, we will be studying about these different friendship levels. And since there are four levels of friendship, we will take two weeks to study each level, learning and then applying what we learn. Just as you start by finding and connecting the edges of a puzzle, the four levels of relationship will serve as the sides of our relationship puzzle in which all the other pieces fit.

Finding fulfilling relationships will be determined by how much you put into practice the truths you learn. You can study for years about how to fly a plane, but until you climb into a cockpit and learn how to fly one, you cannot become a pilot. In much the same way, you can study about how to develop good connections with God and others, but until you begin to apply what you learn, you cannot be a good friend.

Jesus put it like this: "Everyone who hears these words of mine and puts them into practice is like a wise man who built his house on the rock" (Matthew 7:24). If we want to develop rock-solid relationships, we must apply what we learn by putting the truths into practice. Therein lies your challenge for the next eight weeks.

In the words of Julie Andrews, "Let's start at the very beginning . . ."

The first level of friendship could be called **The Stadium**. If you have experienced a concert or a large sporting event, you know what being in a large stadium or arena is like. There's a vast array of people everywhere you look and it can sometimes be quite overwhelming. Like an arena, The Stadium level of relationship is full of people—way too many people to know with any kind of depth. You may have a lot of relationships in The Stadium, but most are fairly shallow—you know a little about everyone and they know a little about you. What they know is common knowledge, known by anyone who knows you. But this is also the level where, out of this large pool of people, you start to make your first connections. The Stadium is *where* relationships start. Now the question is, *how* do they start?

How would you say all relationships begin?

I would suggest that most initial connections start with some kind of *attraction*. You are drawn to another person because something about him or her catches your eye, intrigues you, or makes you want to know more.

Think of a good relationship you currently have. What initially drew you to that person?

Whether it was a smile, tattoos, style, personality, respect, love for animals, generosity, or sense of humor, you sensed something about that person that you admired, resonated with, or aspired to be. That's the initial attraction that triggers every new relationship. Some kind of **CAPTIVATING CHARACTER** sparks in you the desire for potential friendship with another. First Samuel 18:1 says that the soul of Jonathan was "knit to" the soul of David (NKJV). The word *soul* is the Hebrew word *nephesh* and means "desires, character, emotions and thoughts."[1] David and Jonathan developed a friendship because their thoughts, feelings, desires, and overall character were attractive to the other. Conversely, it is difficult to develop a friendship with someone whose attitudes, values, outlook, and behavior are deeply at odds with yours. First Corinthians 15:33 tells us that bad company corrupts good character.

If you have a Bible, open it up and read Jeremiah 31:3. If you don't have a Bible with you, you will always be able to read the Scripture here in the book. How does this Scripture affirm the concept of attraction?

The LORD appeared to us in the past, saying: "I have loved you with an everlasting love; I have drawn you with loving-kindness." — Jeremiah 31:3

---

1. BlueLetterBible.com.

Consider how the concept of attraction applies to your relationship with God. My friendship with God began with attraction. My mother was very loving, nurturing, caring, compassionate, and kind. I was drawn to her. I adored her. I wanted to be just like her. I found that she loved Jesus and sought to live just as He lived. What I was drawn to was not really my mother but rather the characteristics of Jesus Christ that I saw exhibited in her. My mother had introduced me to Jesus through her life, and I was drawn to Him.

Jeremiah 31:3 tells us that we are drawn to Jesus by His loving-kindness. When He is lifted up, all men will be drawn to Him (see John 12:32). I was drawn to Jesus by the loving-kindness exhibited by my mother.

Sadly, many Christians have represented Jesus so poorly that some people are not drawn to Him but are rather repulsed by their distortion of Him. This reality reminds us to be careful to lift up the true character of Jesus in our lives and represent Him well.

Wrapping It Up
Friendship really is about connecting with others who have the captivating character of Jesus displayed throughout their life. So when you approach The Stadium level of relationship, have you made yourself attractive? Are you "God-pretty"? Are you seeking to exemplify the loving-kindness of Jesus that draws people to Him? Is He being lifted up through your life?

Apply It!
Seek Upwardly
Today, write Jeremiah 31:3 in your journal. Throughout your day, refer back to this verse and thank God for His kindness toward you. Write down a couple of ways that God is attractive to you.

Seek Inwardly

Because magnets attract, carry a magnet with you today to remind you of what is so attractive about God and your friends. Let it remind you to be attractive to others by exhibiting Christlike character. Ask God to help you represent Him well, exemplifying His character that when lifted up will draw people to you because they see Him in you. (Beware: If you carry the magnet in your purse, there's no telling *what* you might attract!)

Seek Outwardly

Take some time today to tell your friends the captivating characteristic that attracted you to them initially, especially if it is a characteristic of Jesus. That will give such encouragement to them, and we all need a little of that every once in a while!

Day 2: Beware the Dangers of Destroying

Begin your time with prayer: *Holy Spirit, be my Teacher. Give me understanding on how to put what I learn today into practice. In the name of Jesus I ask, amen.*

．．．．．．．．．

"You never have a second chance to make a first impression." We've all heard it. And we've all met people we were immediately turned off by—people whose first impression couldn't have been worse. Why was that? What was it about those people that made you walk the other way?

Let me suggest a few possibilities:

1. *Self-consciousness.* Many people have been abandoned or wounded in their past and are quite fearful when it comes to venturing out and risking being hurt again. Others may not like who they are because someone rejected them. To protect themselves, they may be quiet, hold things back, or remain closed off. Still others might pose or act disinterested in order to display a level of self-confidence they don't actually feel. They are so self-conscious that they are unable or unwilling to connect.

2. *Self-absorption.* When people are consumed with themselves and their accomplishments and successes, they cannot talk about anything but themselves. The truth is that whatever you are consumed with—whatever is the center of your life—will be what naturally comes out in your conversation. Instead of getting to know another, someone who is self-absorbed monopolizes the conversation and leaves others feeling as though they are not important or interesting.

3. *Selfishness.* Selfish people are always looking for what they can get. If they want to climb the corporate ladder, they only want to use you to get to others who can advance their

career. If they want something from you, they "buddy up" until they get it and then drop you like a hot potato. If they like social media, they will friend you or follow you to increase their own profile. Selfish people use others. They are always looking for what they can gain out of another person, with no real desire for friendship. It is all a quest to get what they want.

So what is the best way to respond to these kinds of people? Open your Bible and read Psalm 139:23-24. How do these verses apply when responding to relationships?

> Search me, O God, and know my heart; test me and know my anxious thoughts. See if there is any offensive way in me, and lead me in the way everlasting. —Psalm 139:23-24

When it comes to friendships, maybe our first question ought to be, "Father, am I self-conscious, self-absorbed, or selfish?" When it comes to relationships, it is always best to do a little self-evaluation before passing judgment on another.

Secondly, we may need to offer someone a second chance because first encounters are usually awkward and nerve-racking. Finally, we need to pray and ask the Spirit to show us if this is a person we need to pursue in friendship. Or perhaps she has the potential to be toxic and we need to wait or move on.

The best perspective to have when meeting someone for the first time is to view her as a Divine Appointment. Since we established that the purpose of friendship is to help one another become holy, we need to meet each person with an understanding that she is important to God and created for a specific purpose. We also need to remember that this encounter could potentially be a friendship God has provided for each of you to help the other find and fulfill the purposes for which He made you. The best way to guard against making a poor first impression and destroying a friendship before it even gets started is to learn to be selfless. Seek to see the person through God's eyes: one that He dearly loves and may intend to be your dearest friend.

God must be the center of relationship because He created it. Without the Creator of friendship in the mix, any attempt to achieve intimacy will be frustrating.

Wrapping It Up

When we are meeting people for the first time in the large arena of The Stadium, we don't want to destroy a friendship before it even starts. The best attitude we can have is to view every new person we meet as a gift from God, with the possibility of the relationship becoming a special friendship in which you help each other become all God originally designed you to be—wholly His.

Apply It!

Seek Upwardly

Create some Divine Appointments with God by setting an alarm on your cell phone (if you have that ability), reminding yourself to talk with Him throughout your day. Thank Him for being your friend. Thank Him for the friends He has given you. Ask Him to remind you that the new people you meet may just be a sweet gift from Him to you. You may even want to draw a gift in your journal and write "look for the gifts of Divine Appointments."

Seek Inwardly

Meditate on Psalm 139:23-24. Write a prayer in your journal, asking the Lord to search out any aspect of your life that is hindering friendships with others. Ask Him to help you be others-focused instead of self-focused. Maybe even draw a pair of glasses in your journal and write "others" across them as a reminder.

Seek Outwardly

Think of ways you can meet new people without being self-conscious, self-absorbed, or selfish. What might you need to say or do? Maybe you could send a note to some of your friends, thanking them for being your friend and for helping you become more like Jesus. Commit to helping them become more like Him as well.

Day 3: Heart Check: Humility

Pray first: *Holy Spirit, be my Teacher. Give me understanding on how to put what I learn today into practice. In the name of Jesus I ask, amen.*

• • • • • • • • •

C. S. Lewis said that humility is not thinking less of yourself but thinking of yourself less.

The Bible tells us that right after Jesus called out His twelve disciples, He sat them down and gave them what has now become commonly known as the Beatitudes (see Matthew 5:1-12). Jesus was basically saying, "Okay, guys, we are about to embark on a journey of sharing the truth with a bunch of people. It will come with its struggles from without and from within. In order for us to keep our focus and remain unified, we will all have to have these kinds of attitudes in order to connect and relate well with others so we can have great impact. So here they are."

Open your Bible and read Matthew 5:1-12.

Now when he saw the crowds, he went up on a mountainside and sat down. His disciples came to him, and he began to teach them, saying:

"Blessed are the poor in spirit,
for theirs is the kingdom of heaven.
Blessed are those who mourn,
for they will be comforted.
Blessed are the meek,
for they will inherit the earth.
Blessed are those who hunger and thirst for righteousness,
for they will be filled.
Blessed are the merciful,
for they will be shown mercy.

Blessed are the pure in heart,
　　for they will see God.
Blessed are the peacemakers,
　　for they will be called sons of God.
Blessed are those who are persecuted because of
　　righteousness,
　　for theirs is the kingdom of heaven.

"Blessed are you when people insult you, persecute you and falsely say all kinds of evil against you because of me. Rejoice and be glad, because great is your reward in heaven, for in the same way they persecuted the prophets who were before you." —Matthew 5:1-12

Jesus began to share these attitudes one by one, and He started with humility.

Why do you think this trait is so important? Record your thoughts in your journal.

As we meet new people whom we are attracted to, viewing them as Divine Appointments from God, a nonnegotiable attitude that we must have is humility. This may be why Jesus started the Beatitudes with this statement: "Blessed are the poor in spirit, for theirs is the kingdom of heaven" (verse 3).

If you go to www.blueletterbible.com, you can look up verses in the Bible and find out their original meaning. Search for the verse and version, and then click on C (for Concordance and Hebrew/Greek Lexicon), and it will give you the original Greek or Hebrew word and its meaning. *Blessed* means "a continual state of happiness; fortunate; blissful." The phrase *poor in spirit* means "destitute, poor, needy and lacking." It is being acutely aware of my helpless and hopeless state apart from God's loving-kindness to me. Picture a beggar on the street, lacking absolutely everything and relying totally on the help of others. If you are poor in spirit, you are spiritually destitute with no hope for surviving without God's help. "Kingdom of heaven" means "the royal power and dignity conferred on Christians in Jesus' kingdom." It is experiencing life under God's kingdom ruling.

Put that together and you get this: I will be fortunate if I am constantly aware that everything I have and everything I am has been given to me out of God's sheer goodness. I am nothing without Him. As I live with that attitude, I will be experiencing what it is like living with God as the King and Ruler of my heart.

Now think about the opposite of the statement.

Here's what you get: Unhappy are those who think they are self-made, self-reliant, and self-sufficient, for they are living as if Satan were ruler of their hearts.

Which attitude of the heart currently best describes you?

Look at the example of Jesus. He had every right to be proud — He was God! Yet He humbled Himself and became a human being to show us how to live, and then He died for our sins (see Philippians 2:5-8). There was not a self-conscious, self-absorbed, or self-centered bone in His body. He was humble and others-focused in every way. If we want to experience positive initial friendships in The Stadium of relationships, the first attitude we need, beautifully exemplified through Jesus and commanded by Jesus, is humility.

Wrapping It Up

Think about a puzzle piece. A humble person is much like a puzzle piece. She is a part of something bigger. She doesn't know exactly what the total picture is quite yet, but once she is joined to the other pieces, life begins to make sense, and together, she and her friends reveal a completed picture. Humility says, "I don't have it all together. I don't know everything, and I need other people in my life to help me complete my life's picture."

Apply It!

Seek Upwardly

Draw a puzzle piece (or find one in your house that you can trace), and write the beatitude from Matthew 5:3 in your journal. You may even want to write the antithesis underneath it. Ask God to help you develop this "poor in spirit" heart of humility within.

Seek Inwardly

Begin to view your new friends with these two thoughts: I wonder what piece of the puzzle I will bring to them to help make them holy and to help them fulfill the purposes for which God created them? I wonder what piece of the puzzle they will bring to me to help make me holy and to help me fulfill the purposes for which God created me?

Seek Outwardly

Put your puzzle piece in a prominent place to be seen throughout your day. You may want to carry it with you. Take time to look at it and thank God for creating you as a specific piece to fit in a bigger puzzle. Ask Him to guide you to friends who He knows will help you complete your puzzle as you help them complete theirs. Since there are four other puzzle pieces that can connect to yours, begin to ask God to reveal to you four key friends He has placed in your life.

Day 4: No Room for Self-Sufficiency

Again today pray these words: *Holy Spirit, be my Teacher. Give me understanding on how to put what I learn today into practice. In the name of Jesus I ask, amen.*

· · · · · · · · ·

Have you ever been to a concert where there were so many people that there was absolutely no room to move? What was that experience like for you?

Just as an arena has no room physically, The Stadium level of relationships has no room for pride, the opposite of humility.

When it comes to relationships, there is no room for some things if you want the relationship to be fulfilling and successful. One thing that will sabotage relationships is self-sufficiency. When we take too much pride in personal success, we begin to believe the lie that we don't need anyone — even God. We think we can do it all by ourselves.

Open your Bible and read Philippians 4:19.

And my God will meet all your needs according to his glorious riches in Christ Jesus. — Philippians 4:19

How does this verse speak against self-sufficiency?

Based on that verse, think about this: If God supplies all our needs, then we must have needs! We are not self-sufficient.

We are a needy people. We need unconditional love, support, encouragement, strength, help, and the list goes on and on. I believe there are two very specific needs that all of humanity has: the need for intimacy and the need for importance. We all have a deep need to be connected to others, to be loved and known. We also have a deep need to make a difference during our time on earth. We want to make some kind of impact that leaves our mark on this world. The truth is that when we walk with God, we find both of those needs met. As we live in deeper relationship with God, we find that He gives us unconditional love and purpose for our lives.

Based on that, here's a question to think about: If God supplies *all* our needs, where do friendships come into play?

When I was a kid, my mother made a *big* deal of birthdays and would always bake a cake for us. I absolutely loved the icing. As a matter of fact, many times I would just lick the icing off and leave the cake for someone else to eat, usually my dad. Now that I am older, my tastes have changed. I absolutely love the cake. As a matter of fact, I usually scrape the icing to the side and eat the cake first. It's the most filling part, with just the perfect amount of sweetness. It satisfies, while at the same time making me hunger for more. I still eat some of the icing, but it is no longer my primary focus; it is just the extra added sweetness that perfectly puts the finishing touches on my treat.

When it comes to relationships, God is the One who meets all our needs. Walking with Him and allowing Him to tell us who He is and who we are is the cake, so to speak. Talking with Him and reading His Word fills the deepest longings in our hearts. It gives us the perfect amount of the sweetness of His love that satisfies our neediness, but it leaves us with a longing for more of Him. Our relationships with others is like the icing. God uses His people to remind us of who He is when hardships in life strike and we forget His presence. Others give a sweet taste of His love as a reminder. They are the icing.

Wrapping It Up

Don't allow self-sufficiency to keep you from meeting and making friends. God made you needy so that you would need Him and others. The best way to keep the right perspective is to remember that God is the sole supplier of all we need, and others are the icing that adds some extra sweetness to the journey.

Apply It!

Seek Upwardly

You may want to draw a cupcake in your journal and write out Philippians 4:19 beside it. Thank God for all the ways He supplies your needs. Write some of those ways in your journal. Express to Him a prominent need that you currently have and ask Him to fill it and to give you the insight to see it when He does.

Seek Inwardly

Ask the Lord to help you see a way (for example, an encouraging note, an act of service, a word of advice) to encourage another by being icing on the cake for her, pointing her to God as her "cake," the Supplier of her needs.

Seek Outwardly

Share with a friend how something she said or did has been icing on the cake for you. For an extra challenge, make a cupcake that you can display somewhere prominent. You may want to gather some girls and bake some cupcakes and explain to them what you are learning.

Day 5: A Promise to Be Made

As you close out your week, start today with our prayer: *Holy Spirit, be my Teacher. Give me understanding on how to put what I learn today into practice. In the name of Jesus I ask, amen.*

* * * * * * * * *

If you look at the life of Jesus, you will see that He often asked people to take action after they saw or received a miracle: "Don't tell anyone" (Luke 5:14). "Go, show yourselves" (Luke 17:14). "Pick up your mat and walk" (John 5:8).

This week we have jumped into our study of relationships, learning that most of them begin with some sort of attraction. We discovered that they can be destroyed before they even start if we are self-centered. The challenge, then, is to view each person as a Divine Appointment, humbly realizing that you are not created to be self-sufficient but that you are a valuable piece of a larger puzzle. We learned to look to God as the ultimate supplier of all we need and discovered that He gives us others as sweet icing on the cake. God gives us friends to enrich this life and to tangibly reveal Himself to us.

As we end this week, the question remains: "What will you do with what you learned? What commitment will you make for the future of your relationships?"

You may be wondering why we have to make commitments. Why not just let it happen naturally, when we're ready or when we feel like it? Commitments are an important action — a reminder and means of accountability to keep the promises we make. Just this morning, the Lord showed me a verse in the Bible that I had never seen before. I want you to read it too.

Open your Bible to Joshua 21:45. How does this verse relate to promises? How is this verse an encouragement to you? You may want to record your thoughts in your journal.

> Not one of all the LORD's good promises to the house of Israel failed; every one was fulfilled. — Joshua 21:45

Isn't it comforting to know that your God has kept *all* His promises? Doesn't it bring great confidence to your relationship with God? In much the same way, you can bring comfort and great confidence to your relationships with others by making a commitment to God to treat others well — to treat them with the same kindness, love, and graciousness that characterizes God's relationship with you.

May I suggest we all make this commitment as we enter The Stadium of friendship?

"I will place attention on God's purpose for everyone I meet."

Commit to focus on the CAPTIVATING CHARACTER of Christ you see in others. Seek to understand how both your friend's character and your character may be puzzle pieces to help each other grow into a person who is wholly God's. Remember to view your friendships as gifts that help point you to God, the One who meets all our needs.

Meditate on this: God has made this same commitment to you: **"I will place attention on My purpose for you."** He focuses His attention on His purposes for you. He constantly places people and circumstances in your life to show you His specific purposes for creating you. When you help your friends see how God is working in their lives to accomplish His purposes, you are partnering with the Lord and following in His footsteps as His disciple.

Wrapping It Up

As you close out your week, ask the Holy Spirit to help you put into practice what you learned; ask in the name of Jesus.

Apply It!

Seek Upwardly

Write this friendship commitment in your journal and refer to it throughout your day and the days to come. Ask God to help you focus not on yourself but rather on others and His purposes for them.

Seek Inwardly

Take some time to write in your journal about what God revealed to you this week. Write about how this has affected your views of God and others and how it might change the way you are living in relationship with God and others.

Seek Outwardly

Share with your friends how they are being used for God's purposes in your life as they demonstrate His character toward you. Write them a note, thanking them for what they mean to you. Let your friends know that you will begin to pray that God uses you to help them fulfill the purposes for which they were created.

the stadium (part 2)

Day 1: Approachable

Pray, *Holy Spirit, be my Teacher. Give me understanding on how to put what I learn today into practice. In the name of Jesus I ask, amen.*

• • • • • • • • •

As a friendship begins to move forward, you will encounter opportunities to get to know each other better. These experiences allow you to see commonalities between the two of you and reveal activities that you can enjoy together. But in order for the friendship to develop, you must become **APPROACHABLE**. What does it mean to be approachable? It starts with a welcoming demeanor, being genuinely open and interested in others. You know approachable people—they are the ones you feel you can talk to about anything.

Consider how this parallels your relationship with God. He is fully approachable. His Word tells us that He welcomes us with open arms, genuinely cares for us because He made us, and wants us to feel free to come to Him with anything. The Bible says that we can go to God with confidence and approach Him with our needs because He loves us and sent Jesus to pay our penalty so we could be in that kind of relationship with Him (see Hebrews 4:16). What a comforting thought that the Creator of the universe is fully approachable to us!

Open your Bible and read Proverbs 18:24. How does this verse relate to being approachable? Summarize it in your own words and then record your thoughts in your journal.

A man who has friends must himself be friendly, but there is a friend who sticks closer than a brother. — Proverbs 18:24, NKJV

You may have heard it said this way: You must be a friend to have a friend. Friendliness is being approachable. It means that as a person gets to know you, she senses a **COMFORTABLE CONNECTION** growing between the two of you. You like each other and like being around each other. Time passes quickly when you are together. Talking together and sitting in silence is comfortable and relaxed. In 1 Samuel 18:1, when it says that Jonathan and David's souls were "knit" together, the writer used the Hebrew word *qashar*, which translates "to bind together." The two friends were developing ties that bound them together. Like puzzle pieces joined together, a comfortable connection was being created between the two men.

For some people, being approachable comes easily. For those who are shy or introverted, this takes more intentionality. So how do we become a friendly person? How do we offer a welcoming demeanor and develop this comfortable connection with others? By talking with others in conversation.

In the movie *The Last Samurai*, a friendship between an American military officer and a Samurai warrior unfolds under some very difficult circumstances. These two men learned how to have conversations on which they built a beautiful friendship that stood strong until the end. Coming from different pasts and different cultures, they found the tools it took to have productive conversations. They found that communication is indeed a work of art. Maybe you can search online for the introduction scene from *The Last Samurai* and watch it today.

When a person paints a beautiful picture, several tools are necessary: a canvas, a palette, paint, and a paintbrush. These tools parallel elements necessary in developing the art of conversation, a critical aspect of deepening relationships.

The canvas represents the environment. If you want to hold a good conversation with someone, it needs to happen in a safe place with few distractions or noises so you don't have to strain to hear one another. A relaxed, comfortable atmosphere helps people let their guard down and feel free to be open.

The palette represents your body language. The way you carry yourself when talking with someone says more than what comes out of your mouth. Eye contact, facial expression, and your posture can indicate whether or not you are interested and engaged. If you are sitting with your arms folded tightly, have a frown on your face, or are looking at something else, you can bet people will not engage you in conversation.

The paint colors represent the various questions you will want to ask another to get to know her better. Some people may be happy to listen all day long and never share anything about themselves. Other people will talk all day and forget to ask any questions of the other person. None will engender a real connection. Here are some great general questions to ask at the beginning of a conversation. They stem from four different areas: family, focus, fun, and faith.

- **Family:** Childhood home? Siblings? Older or younger? Parents? Lived here long? Married? How long? Children? How many? Ages?
- **Focus:** College? Major? Future after graduation? Working? Where? What do you do there? What would you like to be doing?
- **Fun:** Hobbies? Sports? Music? Activities? Shopping? Eating out? Where do you like to eat out? What kinds of books do you like? Movies? Arts?

- **Faith:** Church? Small group? How long? Do you serve somewhere? What are you learning?

Learning to ask good questions, listen to people's answers, and then respond in a respectful tone will help you develop good conversations with others.

Finally, the paintbrush represents listening. The ability to truly listen is an art in itself. Many of us are happy to talk about ourselves but are not very good at listening. That communicates that we are not interested in getting to know others. Part of listening is hearing beyond what a person is saying to understand her heart, the emotions behind the words. You can watch a person's expressions as you listen. The face will often reveal how a person feels about what she is talking about. As she talks, you will see what makes her come alive.

As you listen to a person, a picture of her life unfolds before you. You begin to relate to who she is, where she is in life's journey, and how she thinks and feels. You begin to put yourself in her shoes a bit. You are able to see if there are any common interests on which to build the friendship. It may be an activity, a shared passion and mission, or shared values and priorities. There must be some way of sharing life together for friendship to develop. The more we share together, the richer the friendship.

Now think of this in relation to God. As you approach the One who is fully approachable, you can ask Him questions. You can communicate with Him. You can create an environment to hear Him, talk with Him, ask Him questions, and then listen to His response through His Word, His Spirit, or other people.

Wrapping It Up

If you want to develop a comfortable connection with another person and with God, make yourself approachable by learning the art of conversation. It is key to the longevity and genuineness of friendship.

Apply It!

Seek Upwardly

Write Proverbs 18:24 in your journal. You may even want to post it in a prominent place so you will see it often as a reminder of your study. Ask God to help you become a friendly person with welcoming and hospitable attributes toward others.

Seek Inwardly

Draw a canvas, palette, paint colors, and a paintbrush in your journal and label each one with what it stands for in the art of conversation. Try to remember them in today's conversations with others who cross your path. Apply them as you talk with God as well.

Seek Outwardly

Make your own list of questions you might like to ask to get to know another person. Begin to ask them and see what commonalities you find, maybe even in old friendships.

For some extra fun, call up some girlfriends and go and paint together.

Day 2: Beware the Dangers of Detouring

Pray, *Holy Spirit, be my Teacher. Give me understanding on how to put what I learn today into practice. In the name of Jesus I ask, amen.*

. . . .

Just yesterday I was driving on the highway and saw that the road ahead was as backed up as a clogged drain! I chose to get off the main road to find a detour. Not the best idea. After trying to maneuver through unfamiliar back roads, I found myself in a shabby section of town, completely lost!

Sometimes new friends can go down the wrong path and get obsessed with one another. People meet and get to know each other, finding great commonalities between them. They spend time together, doing things they have in common, and because they enjoy one another, time with each other becomes more and more frequent. Soon their friendship becomes exclusive, keeping others out, especially God.

Sometimes we get so wrapped up in another person that we forget that what attracted us to that person were Christlike characteristics. We forget that the purpose of friendship is to help the other become more like Christ. We let our eyes shift from gratitude toward God for the friendship and Him as the central focus to the friendship itself and how great it makes us feel.

Open your Bible and read Matthew 22:36-40. In your journal, write down how this Scripture can relate to friendship.

"Teacher, which is the greatest commandment in the Law?" Jesus replied: "'Love the Lord your God with all your heart and with all your soul and with all your mind.' This is the first and greatest command-ment. And the second is like it: 'Love your neighbor as yourself.' All the Law and the Prophets hang on these two commandments."
—Matthew 22:36-40

If a friendship does not keep as the focus Jesus and His ultimate purposes, the friendship becomes corrupted. It no longer encourages you to help one another become holy; it does not help you love God more. It does not help you love others because it consumes your time and energy. When the effects of your friendship leave you ignoring the call to love God and others, the friendship is no longer beneficial but erosive.

Wrapping It Up

It is vital that you guard against exclusivity. Something God intended to be so precious can take a serious and dangerous detour when He and others are squeezed out of the friendship.

Apply It!

Seek Upwardly

Write down Matthew 22:37-39. Try to memorize these verses so that you never lose focus of the primary goal of your life and your friendships. Thank God for the friendship and ask for His protection on it. Ask Him to help you keep Him the center of that friendship by showing you how to involve Him in your conversations. Draw a detour sign in your journal and write your prayer, asking God to help your friendships stay on track.

Seek Inwardly

Encourage openness for others to be in friendship with you individually and together with your friends. Allow others to join your circle of friends and encourage your friend to spend time with others without you.

Encourage your friends to live in a deeply loving relationship with God and free them to love others the same way, never interfering with their friendships or stifling them from fulfilling this great commandment.

Ask your friends what the Lord is teaching them and help them see opportunities to reach out to others with love, compassion, kindness, and thoughtfulness.

Seek Outwardly

Make the priority of your life to love the Lord with all your heart and to love and serve others. You may ask your friends to join you, but never let their friendships cause you to sacrifice these two priorities. Write the word *exclusivity* in your journal and draw a big red X over it.

Note: Browse the Internet to find a picture that represents brokenness to you. Put it in your journal to use later.

Day 3: Heart Check: Safety

Pray, *Holy Spirit, be my Teacher. Give me understanding on how to put what I learn today into practice. In the name of Jesus I ask, amen.*

· · · · · · · · ·

Look closely at the picture of brokenness you found yesterday. Write about what you see when you look at it. Ask God to give you insight to see what He wants you to see.

As you make yourself approachable and keep Jesus at the center of your friendships, others will be drawn to you more and more because they see Jesus in you and the relationship is refreshing and freeing. Many people have never experienced this kind of friendship before, so when they find this with you, they may begin to open up to you about things. They may share something to test the waters and see how you respond. They want to know if you are a safe person who is trustworthy, understanding, encouraging, and hopeful. They also want to see if you will reciprocate by sharing honestly about a broken place in your life.

This is where our second beatitude of the heart comes into play. Open your Bible and read Matthew 5:4.

> Blessed are those who mourn, for they will be comforted. — Matthew 5:4

How does this verse relate to our discussion of friendship and communication?

Again, you can go to www.blueletterbible.com and discover what each word of a Scripture verse means. This will prove to be a helpful tool in interpreting the Bible correctly.

We learned last week that *blessed* means "a continual state of happiness; fortunate; blissful." The word *mourn* means "having a godly sorrow that produces change of thought and choices." It means being broken over our sin. We may think of brokenness as a perpetual state of crying and gloom and doom. However, brokenness is an attitude of total dependence on God with no reliance on self, recognizing that living on your own leads to sin and rebellion against God. You are aware of what relying on self has done for you, and you want no part of that. It is total submission to His will and ways in your life. *Comforted* means "forgiveness and salvation." Thus, this beatitude might be summed up as, "Happy and fortunate are those who are broken over the sinful parts of their lives and thus surrender and submit to God, for they will find forgiveness and spiritual growth."

So what would be the opposite of this beatitude?

Perhaps it would be something like this: "Continually unhappy are those who are not sorrowful for their sin, for they will not experience forgiveness or spiritual growth for their lives."

Wrapping It Up

As you and your friend begin to open up about deeper things within, it is important to remember that an attitude of brokenness over your own sin will help you be much more grace-filled and understanding with others. Such vulnerability and transparency in your relationship will help you grow together as you support one another in your brokenness so that the beauty of Christlikeness results. Remember that a key piece of the friendship puzzle is recognizing we are all in this journey of learning to walk with God together, and none of us has fully arrived.

Apply It!

Seek Upwardly

Try to carry your picture around with you today to keep it before you. Thank God for brokenness and for the beauty that can grow through it as we allow Him to work in us. Write today's beatitude (Matthew 5:4) in your journal. You may even want to write the opposite of the verse. Ask God to help you develop this attitude within.

Seek Inwardly

Take some time to bring your broken places to the Lord. Maybe a relationship is broken. Maybe your family is broken. Maybe your heart is broken because of pride, adultery, jealousy, hatred, or bitterness. Bring these things before God and ask Him to heal the broken places in your life. Offer Him a fresh, sweet surrender of your life.

Seek Outwardly

Ask God to help you remember your own broken places so you can see people in that same light and treat them with love, grace, and understanding. Ask God to empower you to help your friends find growth through their broken places.

Day 4: No Room for Being Closed

Pray, *Holy Spirit, be my Teacher. Give me understanding on how to put what I learn today into practice. In the name of Jesus I ask, amen.*

• • • • • • • • • •

Open your Bible and read Numbers 35:1-15. Jot down in your journal what you learn, along with questions you have.

On the plains of Moab by the Jordan across from Jericho, the LORD said to Moses, "Command the Israelites to give the Levites towns to live in from the inheritance the Israelites will possess. And give them pasture-lands around the towns. Then they will have towns to live in and pasturelands for their cattle, flocks and all their other livestock.

"The pasturelands around the towns that you give the Levites will extend out fifteen hundred feet from the town wall. Outside the town, measure three thousand feet on the east side, three thousand on the south side, three thousand on the west and three thousand on the north, with the town in the center. They will have this area as pastureland for the towns.

"Six of the towns you give the Levites will be cities of refuge, to which a person who has killed someone may flee. In addition, give them forty-two other towns. In all you must give the Levites forty-eight towns, together with their pasturelands. The towns you give the Levites from the land the Israelites possess are to be given in proportion to the inheritance of each tribe: Take many towns from a tribe that has many, but few from one that has few."

Then the LORD said to Moses: "Speak to the Israelites and say to them: 'When you cross the Jordan into Canaan, select some towns to be your cities of refuge, to which a person who has killed some-one accidentally may flee. They will be places of refuge from the avenger, so that a person accused of murder may not die before he stands trial before the assembly. These six towns you give will be

your cities of refuge. Give three on this side of the Jordan and three
in Canaan as cities of refuge. These six towns will be a place of refuge
for Israelites, aliens and any other people living among them, so
that anyone who has killed another accidentally can flee there.'"
—Numbers 35:1-15

In Numbers 35:6, we are introduced to the "cities of refuge." In
this chapter, God told Moses to give the tribe of Levi places to live and
pastures for their livestock to graze. The tribe of Levi consisted of the
priests in charge of God's house, the only ones who could approach
God's presence and pray for others. Of these forty-eight towns given
to them, six of these towns were to be "cities of refuge." A city of refuge
was a place where someone who accidentally killed another person
could find safety and protection until he or she could stand trial.

Read Proverbs 18:10: "The name of the LORD is a strong tower;
the righteous run to it and are safe."

What does this verse say about God? How does this verse connect
with the story you read today?

I have found over the course of my life that God is the place I run
to for safety. As Almighty God, my Protector, my Provider, and my
Friend, He is a strong fortress I can run to for safety.

I have also found that God has connected me with people who are
a "city of refuge" for me. They have opened themselves up as a safe
place for me to share my heart without being judged or rejected. They
have given me a place to rest from the pressures of the world and to
protect me from its harm. They have also joined me by praying for me.

If you want to find safe places in God and others, you must
declare that you will not close off from God and others but will press
through the fear to open yourself up. Though past experience may
cause you to be timid about opening up, you must trust God enough
to open up to Him and to the safe ones He places in your life. Isolating
yourself is the surest way to be sucked into depression and despair.

Make no room for being closed. Open your heart to God and connect to safe people, and you will find a new breath of life as God and others partner with you in your journey.

Wrapping It Up

Just as the Levites provided a safe place that was always open and approachable, God provides that same safety in Himself and others. Just as the Levites had pastureland on which to graze, God gives us Himself and friends who offer us comfort to graze upon in our times of need. And just as the Levites joined the people to God through their prayers for them, God connects us with friends who are committed to join us in praying for our relationship with God.

Apply It!

Seek Upwardly

Draw a picture of a tower in your journal. Write Proverbs 18:10 above it. Around your tower, write various names of God that give you strength, protection, and safety. Here are a few: Mighty God, Prince of Peace, Wonderful Counselor, and Friend. Take a moment to simply thank God for who He is. Then pick one of His names that you need for today and take it with you wherever you go to remind you that God is a strong tower of safety.

Seek Inwardly

Think about who may need you to be a city of refuge for them. What might that look like for you? Ask God to reveal opportunities you might have this week or even this day to offer your friendship as a city of refuge for another.

Seek Outwardly

Send a thank-you note to a special friend who has been like a sheltering tree when you've needed one. If you have never had a friend like that, ask God to send you a friend who can be that for you.

Day 5: A Promise to Be Made

Pray, *Holy Spirit, be my Teacher. Give me understanding on how to put what I learn today into practice. In the name of Jesus I ask, amen.*

. . . .

This week it is my prayer that you have come to know in a deeper sense that God is fully APPROACHABLE and that you can have a COMFORTABLE CONNECTION with your heavenly Father as He offers you peace, protection, and safety in Him. I also pray that you have begun to see the importance of being a friend who offers the same to others in friendship.

Open your Bible and read 2 Corinthians 1:3-4. Can you think of a time when God has brought comfort to you? Can you think of a time when God used someone else to comfort you during a difficult time in your life?

> Praise be to the God and Father of our Lord Jesus Christ, the Father of compassion and the God of all comfort, who comforts us in all our troubles, so that we can comfort those in any trouble with the comfort we ourselves have received from God. — 2 Corinthians 1:3-4

As we find ourselves at the end of the week, you must again ask yourself these questions: "What will I do with what I have learned? What commitment will I make for the future of my relationships?"

When God makes Himself fully approachable to you, when you have experienced the art of conversation with Him, and when you have found comfort and safety in Him, you really have no other response but to pass on what you have received, because you know how special it was to you. You can experience deep joy in comforting others as you have been comforted yourself.

You can begin to foster safety in your relationships through a commitment to God about how you will treat others with this gift of friendship that He has given you. May I suggest we all make this commitment as we continue to walk in The Stadium of friendship?

"I will pass on what I have received."

This means that you will commit to pass on the Christlike trait of compassion, offering a safe place of comfort because you have been comforted.

Meditate on this: God has made this same commitment to you: **"I will pass on what I have received."**

In John 15:15, Jesus said, "I have called you friends, for everything that I learned from my Father I have made known to you." When you provide a safe place for your friends, you are partnering with the Lord in what He is doing in the lives of your friends. You are following in His footsteps by doing just what He did. You are living as His disciple.

Wrapping It Up

In closing, ask the Holy Spirit to help you put into practice what you have learned this week; ask in the name of Jesus.

Apply It!

Seek Upwardly

Write this friendship commitment in your journal and refer to it throughout your day and the days to come. Ask God to help you pass on what has been given to you.

Seek Inwardly

Take some time to write in your journal about what God revealed to you this week. How has this affected the way you view your relationships with God and others, and how will it change the way you live in relationship?

Seek Outwardly

Share with a friend how she has comforted and encouraged you during a difficult time in your life. Write her a note or text her, thanking her for what she means to you. Let your friend know that you will begin to pray that God will use you to comfort her when she is in need.

week 3

the cover-up (part 1)

Day 1: Available

Pray, *Holy Spirit, be my Teacher. Give me understanding on how to put what I learn today into practice. In the name of Jesus I ask, amen.*

. . . .

If you've seen *The Phantom of the Opera*, you know of the horrific discovery made when Christine removes the mask of Erik. When she unmasks him and beholds his face, Erik goes into a panicked frenzy, crawling away and crying, fearing she will leave him.

One of the scariest places to be in a relationship is when your friend invites you to remove your masks. Masks are the means by which you cover up the parts of your life that only you know and would prefer to keep covered up for fear that their exposure will warrant rejection. We all have masks, and yet we all long to be fully known by another and fully accepted and loved. For the next two weeks, we will discuss our next level of friendship, **The Cover-Up**, and explore ways to begin to drop our masks with our friends so we can truly heal and grow.

Many friendships will come to a standstill unless you are both willing to start uncovering deeper aspects of yourselves to the other. But this will be a process. You (or your friend) may have experienced a deep wound from someone who turned out to be untrustworthy and betraying.

Because of this, becoming more transparent will take time and patience. It will require that you become **AVAILABLE** to your friends. This means that you will make spending time with them a priority; you will be mindful and intentional about having quality time with them.

Again, think about how this trait parallels your relationship with Jesus. Doesn't it bring you comfort to know that He is always accessible to us? He is readily available whenever we need or want Him. There is no need to try to hide anything from Him because He already knows everything about you anyway. You can take every mask off and know that He is fully accepting and loving.

Open your Bible and read Hebrews 4:13-16. What do these verses tell you about approaching God? Record your thoughts in your journal.

Nothing in all creation is hidden from God's sight. Everything is uncovered and laid bare before the eyes of him to whom we must give account.

Therefore, since we have a great high priest who has gone through the heavens, Jesus the Son of God, let us hold firmly to the faith we profess. For we do not have a high priest who is unable to sympathize with our weaknesses, but we have one who has been tempted in every way, just as we are — yet was without sin. Let us then approach the throne of grace with confidence, so that we may receive mercy and find grace to help us in our time of need.
—Hebrews 4:13-16

Verse 13 tells us that "nothing in all creation is hidden from God's sight. Everything is uncovered and laid bare before the eyes of him to whom we must give account." There is great peace and security in knowing that God cares enough about us to see us at all times. But to think that He sees all the sinful yuck in my life can be unsettling unless I remember that when He sees me, He sees the blood of His Son covering me. Jesus paid the penalty for my sin, so I no longer bear it. My sin is forgiven and gone! That gives me reason to thank Him and praise Him for loving me that much. Who wouldn't want to have a relationship with such a wonderful Friend? And who wouldn't willfully take off every mask before such a loving One? He is a Friend who is always available for us. We can bring Him our joys, sorrows, concerns, and sin. He will rejoice with us, turn our weeping into laughter, take care of our worries, and forgive our sin.

What do you need to bring to Him?

If you want to bring that aspect of God's character into your friendships, you must open yourself up to **CONSISTENT ENCOUNTERS** with others. In many cases, friends who do not spend time together do not remain friends for very long. Friendship takes time, and healthy friends are excited to be with each other and feel encouraged when they are together. They talk, laugh, and cry, connecting in ways unique to both of them. Spending time with your friend on a consistent basis and being intentional about growing together will give both of you the confidence to slowly but surely remove your relational masks and begin to reveal deep places in you that no one else may know. The questions you began with in your initial conversations (see page 39) will move to a deeper level, involving your opinions, your goals, your thoughts, your feelings, and your desires. These questions may also grow into conversations about a current difficulty you are experiencing or a troubling time you went through in your past that has had a direct effect on your life. Friendships that deepen to The Cover-Up level have a never-ending conversation, an ongoing dialogue that just picks back up with each time spent together.

Wrapping It Up

If you want to take your friendships to the next level, make yourself available by developing consistent encounters with your friends, freeing them to lower the masks they may never before have removed. Such vulnerability is critical in creating an environment for the unveiling of oneself in friendship.

Apply It!

Seek Upwardly

Revelation 3:20 says, "Look! I stand at the door and knock. If you hear my voice and open the door, I will come in, and we will share a meal together as friends" (NLT). Write this verse in your journal and thank your heavenly Father for always being available for you. Thank Him for seeing all of you, both the good and the bad, and loving you just the same. Draw a picture of a door. Ask the Lord to help you not be closed but rather open to Him, as well as to others.

Since relationships take time, be intentional about spending time talking with God today. Tell Him how awesome you think He is and listen for Him to speak to you. He has a lot of loving things to say.

Seek Inwardly

Think about the people God has placed in your life. With whom do you feel God wants you to remove your masks? Are you willing? Why or why not? Dialogue with God about this and let Him help you press through your fears and find love and acceptance in a safe friend.

Seek Outwardly

Ask the Holy Spirit to reveal to you the friend or friends to whom you need to make yourself more available. Begin to intentionally plan some time together. Invite them to join you for everyday activities, such as shopping or running errands. Also, find some time to sit for coffee and give each other some undivided attention.

Ask the Holy Spirit to help you be the first to begin removing your masks. This action gives others the courage to do the same. If they do not join you, then wait and continue to invest in the friendships until they are ready. If they remain closed, the door for a growing friendship with them is being closed. Be thankful God revealed this and seek out another friendship.

Day 2: Beware the Dangers of Deception

Pray, *Holy Spirit, be my Teacher. Give me understanding on how to put what I learn today into practice. In the name of Jesus I ask, amen.*

· · · · · · · · ·

Take a second to go online to check out some optical illusions. You've likely heard the phrase "looks can be deceiving." The very nature of optical illusions is to trick the eyes into seeing something that's not real. Our eyes deceive us into thinking something that defies natural logic.

Spiritually, we can experience the same thing. We can look at something and think we see one thing, while it is altogether something else. It's a deception. It's a cover-up. The word *deception* means "a misleading act or falsehood." By the very nature of the definition, people don't know they are being misled. Usually deception is unintentional. Deception comes from Satan, the great deceiver, who likes nothing better than to cover up the truth with a lie.

Deception can creep into friendships as well. If you are not careful, one of you could be deceived into thinking that the other has all the answers and can fix all your problems. This is the great deception that began with Eve.

Open your Bible and read Genesis 3:1-6. What was Eve deceived into thinking?

> Now the serpent was more crafty than any of the wild animals the LORD God had made. He said to the woman, "Did God really say, 'You must not eat from any tree in the garden'?"
>
> The woman said to the serpent, "We may eat fruit from the trees in the garden, but God did say, 'You must not eat fruit from the tree that is in the middle of the garden, and you must not touch it, or you will die.'"
>
> "You will not surely die," the serpent said to the woman. "For God knows that when you eat of it your eyes will be opened, and you will be like God, knowing good and evil."

> When the woman saw that the fruit of the tree was good for
> food and pleasing to the eye, and also desirable for gaining wisdom,
> she took some and ate it. She also gave some to her husband, who
> was with her, and he ate it. — Genesis 3:1-6

Satan deceived Eve into thinking that eating the fruit would make her whole and perfect, just like God. You see, Satan wears his own mask, making himself look good when he is altogether evil in every way. Second Corinthians 11:14 says, "Satan himself masquerades as an angel of light." Satan deceived Eve into thinking that God was withholding something good from her; she became convinced that she should eat of the fruit of the tree that God had forbidden. Her desires, coupled with the Enemy's deception, took her down a deadly path.

When it comes to friendships, this same scenario can take place. We begin to take off our masks with a friend. She offers us grace and mercy and may even weep with us in compassion and empathy. She may even take up an offense by seeking to fix what is broken, giving great advice, and supporting you as you walk out what she encouraged you to do. None of that is bad in and of itself, unless that friend begins to take the place of God in your life! If you are not careful with who owns your heart, you will be deceived into thinking that you don't need God because you have your friend. If that happens, you will run to that friend for everything instead of relying on God.

Putting a friend in a space that should be reserved for God is like trying to force a puzzle piece into a place where it doesn't belong. This is a very dangerous place to be. Your friend is just as limited as you. God was pretty adamant when He said that He would have no other gods before Him. That's exactly what a friend can become when you begin to run to her instead of Him.

Here's how you can guard against this deceptive trap:

- Always consider God as the main source for life, love, and help. Remember, He is the cake and your friend is simply the icing. He is the final authority in your life. He is the One to seek and to obey because He created you and knows you better than anyone. His counsel is the purest, wisest, and best.

- Always keep your friend in proper perspective. Whatever kindness, compassion, grace, mercy, and love you receive is possible because Your Father gave her the ability to offer those gifts to you. James 1:17 says that every good and perfect gift comes from God, so the endearing qualities you see in your friend is actually Jesus living through her. Those traits are not meant to draw you closer to a friend and further from your Father but rather closer and closer to the Father as you see Him made evident through a friend who helps you in your time of need. It always begins and ends with your loving Father.

Wrapping It Up

The Enemy can create deception and distortion even in the most precious of friendships, making them the source of life instead of your Father. Guard your heart and your friendships from the destruction of the Enemy by making your Creator Daddy the supreme source for love, encouragement, direction, comfort, and guidance. View anything your friends contribute as evidence that God lives in them and God loves you enough to work through them to help you.

Apply It!

Seek Upwardly

In your journal, draw a face on the left side of the page and write *deception* where the eyes would go. Ask God to protect you from being deceived into believing that someone is more important than He is. On the right side of the page draw a totem pole and write from top to bottom the priorities of relationship that are currently in your life.

Ask God to help you keep your relationships in the right priority, with Him being first and all others following Him.

Seek Inwardly

Write John 14:6 on a notecard: "I am the way and the truth and the life." Carry this with you today to remind you that God is your source for all you need. What do you need to say or do that will keep your focus on Jesus as your source? If you struggle with relying on people, why do you think that is? What can you do about that?

Seek Outwardly

Constantly bring Jesus into your conversations. When a friend does or says something Christlike, don't compliment her for what she did, but bring honor and praise to God by telling her that she reflected Jesus in her words and actions.

Seek to be like Jesus to your friend. When you are given a compliment, simply offer it back to God as the source of your kindness, grace, mercy, and love. I have often seen an ice skater gather the roses thrown to her and take them to her coach in honor. When you receive praise and turn it back to Jesus, you honor the One who gave you the ability to be a good friend to another. This practice will keep the relationship in balance and guard against the deception of the Enemy that causes us to forget God.

Day 3: Heart Check: Teachable, Trainable, and Moldable

Pray, *Holy Spirit, be my Teacher. Give me understanding on how to put what I learn today into practice. In the name of Jesus I ask, amen.*

• • • • • • • • •

If you have some modeling clay around the house, go grab it. Work it with your hands as you read today's study.

When I was a kid, I loved to create. From sand castles at the beach to mud pies in the backyard, creating something from nothing with my hands was amazing to me. The best creative time I had indoors was with Play-Doh. My very favorite Play-Doh experience was when we had a Play-Doh hair studio. I crammed the Play-Doh into the person, turned a crank, and the bald person grew Play-Doh hair! It was hilarious! My mom was not a fan of Play-Doh, especially when I got it on my tennis shoes and smeared it into her carpet. That was when my career as a beautician came to an end.

As the relational masks begin to come down and you begin to spend consistent time together with a friend, it is vital that you both maintain a moldable and teachable spirit. Remembering that none of us is perfect and none of us has all the answers helps us run to the One who does. You will not have all the answers for your friend and she will not have all the answers for you. If your friend could answer every longing, every question, and every prayer for you, you wouldn't need Jesus! God is a jealous God who wants your total allegiance and devotion. He will never allow someone to meet all your needs because if she did, she would take His place in your life, and He loves you too much to let that happen.

Jesus taught His disciples an attitude of the heart that keeps us grounded with a proper perspective of ourselves and others.

Open your Bible and read Matthew 5:5. What trait did Jesus describe? How does this trait encourage positive friendships? Record your thoughts in your journal.

> Blessed are the meek, for they will inherit the earth. — Matthew 5:5

We now know what *blessed* means (see page 27), so let's examine these other words. The word *meek* means "power under control; trainable like breaking a horse; a lack of resistance to God's discipline that promotes growth." Meekness is a disposition that helps us accept God's dealings with us as a means to purify us and make us the person He created us to be. Therefore, in meekness we don't resist Him or argue with Him but rather trust Him completely. It means that though you have a lot of power within you to respond however you want to in any given situation, that power is submitted to the leadership of God. When God is showing you areas in your life that do not please Him, meekness in you will not resist His instruction. Rather, you will surrender that area of your life to Him to forgive, remove, and restore. A wild horse has a power that is out of control until he is broken and a bit is placed in his mouth. We are also out of control until we allow God to break us and reign (like a rein) over us.

Notice the progression that Jesus was showing His disciples. As we humble ourselves before Him (poor in spirit) and are broken from all self-reliance (mourn), He is able to put a rein on our hearts to begin to lead us. This means trusting His ways fully and understanding that even bad things will be used by Him for our good. Romans 8:28 says, "We know that in all things God works for the good of those who love him, who have been called according to his purpose." The phrase "inherit the earth" is speaking of the new earth that God will create for those who are saved, after He returns and destroys this current earth. God has found you responsible enough to receive a portion of the land for your inheritance.

Isn't being teachable at the very heart of being a disciple? A disciple by its very nature is one who is a student and follower of Jesus, watching His ways and following Him. If we truly want to be a disciple of Jesus, we will humble ourselves, remain in a broken state of total dependence on Him, and maintain a teachable spirit that opens ourselves to His molding of us.

Think about the clay you have. What would happen if you left it out? The clay would dry out. In the same way, when our lives are lived outside the molding hands of God, our hearts and lives dry up. Life becomes a series of purposeless events with highs and lows instead of a surrender to the Potter's hands, where Christlikeness is shaped.

So we might paraphrase this verse to say, "Fortunate and happy are those who surrender to God's control, for they will receive an inheritance as His child."

Now consider the opposite: "Continually unhappy are those who refuse to be taught and do not trust in God's goodness in all things, for they will not receive any inheritance in the life to come."

Wrapping It Up

Spending time with God and others through continual encounters allows you to begin to take off your cover-ups and bare all of yourself. But in order for growth to take place in those areas, you must let God reveal His truth and let safe friends help you. You cannot resist God's molding hand that wants to convict you, teach you, or lead you. God will also use your friends to speak truth to you and encourage you, and you must let them. If you are going to remove your masks and encourage others to do the same, you will have to learn to be teachable, continually asking God, "What do You want me to learn through this situation?" In that way, you are trusting that He has good purposes for you, and your attentiveness and response to those purposes will grow you into the person He created you to be.

Apply It!

Seek Upwardly

Write Matthew 5:5 in your journal and ask God to grow this attitude within your heart. Also, try to memorize Romans 8:28. Throughout your day, continually acknowledge that every circumstance you encounter can be an opportunity for God to teach you something, using even the hard times for your good. Thank Him for having your best interests at heart and for loving you enough to work all things for your good. Remind yourself to trust that His heart toward you is good. In this way, you partner with God to complete His work in you and place yourself as clay in the Potter's hands.

Seek Inwardly
You may want to draw a ruler and write *teachable* beside it. Take a teachable attitude into the friendships God has placed in your life. Many times, God will use your friends to help you grow, but you must maintain a teachable spirit to receive and embrace that growth. Remind yourself that even if your friends say something that is harsh or somewhat critical and offensive, their heart toward you is good.

Seek Outwardly
Place yourself in a position to learn something new. Take that same teachable spirit into your relationships. When your friends share a once masked area with you, temper your response so they understand that your heart toward them is good. If you have an opportunity to teach them, applaud them for being teachable. Make sure you teach them in a humble and broken way, being fully aware that you are on this journey of learning alongside them. This will create a beautiful partnership for each of you to grow into Christlikeness.

Day 4: No Room for Self-Exaltation

Pray, *Holy Spirit, be my Teacher. Give me understanding on how to put what I learn today into practice. In the name of Jesus I ask, amen.*

• • • • • • • • •

I once heard a story about a man who went into the woods and found a beautiful tree. The grain of this tree was absolutely perfect for his keen ability to carve and whittle. He cut down the tree and took the large log of wood back to his home. There, he split the wood and carved an exquisite piece of art. He burned the rest of the wood in a fire, warming himself and cooking his food to nourish himself. Day after day he praised his piece of art. He told others about it. He brought others to see it. He sat before it day and night, admiring his handiwork. He began to consider it a good luck piece for him. Over time, he began sitting in front of it and asking it to save him from his enemies. He began to bow down to it and worship it.

This story sounds so ridiculous! Who in his right mind would consider half of a piece of wood worth creating something to worship, while using the other piece to burn in a fire? Can half of the same piece of wood be considered valuable while discarding the other? Why would anyone worship something that he created himself?

This story seems so silly, but it actually originates in Scripture. Open your Bible and read Isaiah 44:9-20. See what the Holy Spirit reveals to you. Write down your thoughts in your journal.

> All who make idols are nothing,
>   and the things they treasure are worthless.
> Those who would speak up for them are blind;
>   they are ignorant, to their own shame.
> Who shapes a god and casts an idol,
>   which can profit him nothing?

He and his kind will be put to shame;
    craftsmen are nothing but men.
Let them all come together and take their stand;
    they will be brought down to terror and infamy.

The blacksmith takes a tool
    and works with it in the coals;
he shapes an idol with hammers,
    he forges it with the might of his arm.
He gets hungry and loses his strength;
    he drinks no water and grows faint.
The carpenter measures with a line
    and makes an outline with a marker;
he roughs it out with chisels
    and marks it with compasses.
He shapes it in the form of man,
    of man in all his glory,
    that it may dwell in a shrine.
He cut down cedars,
    or perhaps took a cypress or oak.
He let it grow among the trees of the forest,
    or planted a pine, and the rain made it grow.
It is man's fuel for burning;
    some of it he takes and warms himself,
    he kindles a fire and bakes bread.
But he also fashions a god and worships it;
    he makes an idol and bows down to it.
Half of the wood he burns in the fire;
    over it he prepares his meal,
    he roasts his meat and eats his fill.
He also warms himself and says,
    "Ah! I am warm; I see the fire."

From the rest he makes a god, his idol;
  he bows down to it and worships.
He prays to it and says,
  "Save me; you are my god."
They know nothing, they understand nothing;
  their eyes are plastered over so they cannot see,
  and their minds closed so they cannot understand.
No one stops to think,
  no one has the knowledge or understanding to say,
"Half of it I used for fuel;
  I even baked bread over its coals,
  I roasted meat and I ate.
Shall I make a detestable thing from what is left?
  Shall I bow down to a block of wood?"
He feeds on ashes, a deluded heart misleads him;
  he cannot save himself, or say,
  "Is not this thing in my right hand a lie?" — Isaiah 44:9-20

Verse 20 says that man's mind is deluded or deceived; his heart has deceived him. Because of the deception, he cannot discern, "Is not this thing in my right hand a lie?"

God created us for relationship, first with Himself and then with others. When we take the beauty of friendship and try to make it more than it was intended to be, we have made it an idol. We have set up the friendship to save us from our bad circumstances or enemies and to be our source of help. We've begun to worship the created instead of the Creator.

Take heed! When you become someone's friend, you have been given a precious privilege from the Father. It is a gift from your Daddy. But make no mistake about it: When you begin to exalt yourself as the best friend who has all the answers, who can fix every problem, and who can mend every broken place, you have set yourself up as an idol to be worshipped. Without ever saying a word, you have communicated that your friend doesn't need God—she just needs you. You have deceived your friend into this mind-set, and your friend has no idea that the friendship she is exalting has become an idol. And God will destroy the friendship if it takes His place.

If this truth feels heavy to you, it is because it is. Many friendships have become so distorted that they become enmeshed together, not knowing where one person ends and the other begins. This is mere steps away from crossing the line to an inappropriate relationship. Unhealthy relationships start innocently but can quickly turn toxic, and before you know it, you are wondering how in the world you got to this point. Beware! Enjoy your friendships, but keep them in balance.

Wrapping It Up

Friendships can add a dimension to our lives that is delightful and nourishing to our souls; however, they must remain within the boundaries for which God created them. As you make yourself more and more available to one another, make Jesus the center and the source. Do not exalt yourself in relationships—that place was never yours to take.

Apply It!

Seek Upwardly

Write these two Scripture verses in your journal: "For whoever exalts himself will be humbled, and whoever humbles himself will be exalted" (Matthew 23:12) and "Now as always Christ will be exalted in my body" (Philippians 1:20). Ask God to help you exalt Him as the source of life and help and hope. Thank Him that He is both your and everyone else's source of life. Ask God to help you better understand humility and to keep you humble, never exalting yourself above Him in another's life.

Seek Inwardly

Write the word *idol* in your journal and mark a big X over it. Both declare and commit to God that He is your only source for life and that you will choose Him first every time. Ask Him to give you wisdom to know when to seek counsel from a trusted and safe friend and when to take a few steps back in relationship when someone is becoming more attached than she needs to be. Consider how easy it is for unhealthy attachments to take place so that you can be more understanding and helpful with others.

Seek Outwardly

Give God credit for anything good that you are able to give a friend. Constantly remind friends that it is Christ in you that they see, not anything in and of yourself apart from Him.

Day 5: A Promise to Be Made

Pray, *Holy Spirit, be my Teacher. Give me understanding on how to put what I learn today into practice. In the name of Jesus I ask, amen.*

• • • • • • • • •

It has been my prayer throughout this week that you have seen that God is your best friend. No one could ever be and do what God can be and do for you. My prayer is that you have seen that He is constantly AVAILABLE to you and longs to have CONSISTENT ENCOUNTERS with you. I hope you have determined to discipline yourself to spend time with God each day, just the two of you, and to talk with Him throughout your day as well. This builds a depth to your friendship with Him that gives you confidence and safety in His presence with you. I also pray that you have begun to see the importance of being a friend who is available to others.

Has God ever shown you a verse from His Word in your time together, only to meet up later with a friend who needed that verse to encourage or challenge her?

Open your Bible and read John 16:13. How does this verse relate to helping friends in need?

> But when he, the Spirit of truth, comes, he will guide you into all truth. He will not speak on his own; he will speak only what he hears, and he will tell you what is yet to come. — John 16:13

Jesus has never covered up. He has offered Himself in complete vulnerability all the way to full disclosure and exposure on a cross. His Spirit guides us into all truth, where there are no lies, no masks, and no need to cover up.

As we develop consistent encounters with the Father, He guides us into the truths we need and even truths that our friends need. He not only makes Himself available, but He also makes His Word available to us, providing the right words to give our friends. We don't have to give them our own words, which are limited, biased, and bent, but we give them truth from the Truth Giver that will help them.

You can begin to guard against self-exaltation and unhealthy dependency in your relationships by making a commitment to God about how you will treat others with this gift of friendship that He has given you.

May I suggest we all make this commitment as we continue to remove our Cover-Ups in friendship?

"I will always point my friends to Jesus, not myself."

This commitment means that you will point your friends to the true source of life.

So how do you do this? When a friend tells you about a situation and wants your advice, ask her these questions: (1) Have you prayed and asked God to show you what to do? (2) What does His Word say about this? At this point the Lord may give you a verse you can share with her. If you both still have no clarity about the situation after you have asked these questions, then commit to pray about the situation and let her know what the Lord says to you about it. This will keep it pointed in the right direction, to the right source.

Another part of this commitment is the discipline of gathering every accolade others give you and offering them as evidence of Jesus living in you. All the glory goes back to the source. Finally, this commitment means you will be an available person who spends consistent time with her Father and her friends, maintaining a teachable spirit to learn and grow into kingdom living.

Now think about this: God has made this same commitment to you: **"I will always point you to Myself."**

Jesus said, "But the Counselor, the Holy Spirit, whom the Father will send in my name, will teach you all things and will remind you of everything I have said to you" (John 14:26). That's a promise we can stake our lives on as we remain meek and teachable. When you keep this posture in friendship, you partner with the Lord in what He is doing in the lives of your friends and follow in His footsteps as His disciple by doing just what He did.

Wrapping It Up

As you close this time, ask the Holy Spirit to help you put into practice what you learned this week; ask in the name of Jesus.

Apply It!

Seek Upwardly

Write this friendship commitment in your journal and refer to it throughout your day and the days to come. Ask God to help you point others to Him.

Seek Inwardly

Take some time to write in your journal about what stuck out to you as God revealed Himself to you this week. Write down how this truth has affected your relational views of God and others, as well as how it has changed the way you are living in relationship with God and others.

Seek Outwardly

Make yourself available to a friend who may need to pull down her mask. Give her the freedom to uncover places in her life. Receive what she shares with an intent to learn from her and from God. Point her to Jesus and His Word as the answer. Never exalt yourself but only Jesus as the only One who can really help her.

week 4

the cover-up (part 2)

Day 1: Accepting

Pray, *Holy Spirit, be my Teacher. Give me understanding on how to put what I learn today into practice. In the name of Jesus I ask, amen.*

. . . .

There is nothing worse than taking your makeup off and someone saying, "Wow, you look *very* different!" What do you do with that statement? If it is a compliment, then my makeup looks terrible. If it is a criticism, then you can bet I will wear makeup wherever I go for the rest of my life!

Last week we talked about making ourselves available to others. Availability will open the door for relational masks to come down. When those cover-ups do come down, your response is critical to the transformation of your friend. If she shares something deep within and you reject her or respond with disbelief or pride, she may run so far into a cave of shame that she'll never dare to come out again. That is why at this point in your friendship you need to be **ACCEPTING.**

Acceptance is difficult for many of us because we don't know how to respond to people who do or say things that they know they shouldn't or that we think we would never do or say. Yet God tells us to offer acceptance.

Open your Bible and read Romans 15:7. How does this verse challenge us in our relationships?

> Accept one another, then, just as Christ accepted you, in order to bring praise to God. — Romans 15:7

The word *accept* comes from the original Greek word *receive* and means "to take in as one's friend and companion; to take by the hand and lead; to take in and show kindness."

A biblical understanding of acceptance means that when your friend takes off the cover-up and reveals deep, hurtful places within her, you need to receive that unveiling with mercy. She needs you to consider how she must feel and then help her find God's truth and God's plan for healing and growth in her life. You must seek the Lord to show you what piece of the puzzle you will be in helping her find this truth and healing.

Our acceptance of others grows in proportion to our understanding of God's acceptance of us through Christ Jesus. He receives us as we are with all our sin and shame. He forgives us, cleanses us, and leads us into a life that brings Him honor. We don't have to be perfect. We don't need to get our lives together enough to come to God. We can come to Him just as we are and allow Him to change us as we walk with Him. What a gift. And if we have been so graciously given such a gift, how can we not offer that gift to someone else?

As the masks come down and the flaws are revealed, we must be a friend who demonstrates **CONSIDERATE ACCEPTANCE**. Consideration means we give careful thought to the feelings and circumstances of others *before* we react and respond. It means taking a moment to put ourselves in another's shoes, walking in them long enough to think about what that person's life is like. When we do this, we are able to accept others where they are and help them along their journey.

Sometimes when the cover-ups are dropped, lies can be revealed. When your friend shares a deep wound or sin in her life, the Spirit may help you see a lie she is believing as truth, one that needs to be eradicated and replaced with God's truth. Part of friendship is reminding others of the truth and helping them break free of the agreement they have made with a lie they are believing. You can help others accept God's truth about how He sees them and the good He can bring in the midst of their circumstances.

As friendship is reciprocated, you, too, will be faced with the need to be transparent and to expose lies that you have been believing. You must also seek the truth about what God says and allow your friends to help you break free of those lies. You must let friends speak God's truth over your life and accept that truth, even when it is hard or difficult to believe because it doesn't feel true. Just because we don't feel that something is truthful doesn't cease to make it truthful. We must accept it whether we believe it or not. Acceptance of each other and acceptance of God's truth are essential components to spiritual growth and healing in your and another person's life.

In the selfish generation in which we live, we often forget to consider how our actions and words will affect another person. As a result, there are a lot of wounded people who are afraid to reach out in friendship. Because of this, many relationships stall. We must learn to consider others and accept them just the way they are, even if we disagree with their decisions or are turned off by their behavior. We must also accept God's truth about us and seek to help our friends know and accept God's truth about them.

Wrapping It Up

If we want deep, meaningful friendships that help us take off the masks and move past our hurts into the freedom and joy that Christ offers, we must start by being considerate of others. When their makeup is removed, we have to consider their feelings before we respond. We must accept others and help them accept what God says about them no matter how they feel about themselves. We must ask God to help us give His truth away and also accept His truth for ourselves.

Apply It!

Seek Upwardly

Take some time to write Romans 15:7 in your journal and then draw a mask. Consider God's acceptance of you. Thank God that you can take off your mask and know that you are completely accepted by Him even when you have been rejecting Him. Ask God to help you be as accepting of others as He has been of you.

Seek Inwardly

Ask God to help you become a considerate person. Ask Him to help you think about how your actions will affect others *before you respond* to their stories. Ask Him to help you consider your friends as they reveal struggles with sin and shame, allowing you to step into their shoes long enough to understand them better. Finally, ask God to reveal truth to you regarding areas in which you are believing lies about yourself; ask Him to help you accept His truth in spite of how you feel.

Seek Outwardly

Ask God to show you one truth that a friend needs to hear today from His Word. Find the Scripture that supports that truth and pass it on to your friend with the phrase, "Accept it because it is true!" You may want to find a funny or goofy song (such as "You Are My Sunshine") and video record yourself singing or lip-synching it. Then send it to your friend as a cheerful reminder of who God says she is! (Part of letting go of the cover-ups is acting goofy and being able to laugh at yourself!) Make sure you put the attention on God's thoughts toward her, not just your own.

Day 2: Beware the Dangers of Differentiation

Pray, *Holy Spirit, be my Teacher. Give me understanding on how to put what I learn today into practice. In the name of Jesus I ask, amen.*

. . . .

In December of 1988, the movie *Beaches* debuted in theaters all over America. It got its fame from the theme song "Wind Beneath My Wings," which won Record of the Year and Song of the Year at the 1990 Grammy Awards. The story is about two very different girls raised in two different environments and how their friendship remained through many difficult circumstances. One of the struggles they had was a constant comparison of one to the other. It almost destroyed their friendship.

One behavior that detours a friendship is the comparison game. Comparing yourself to a friend can produce one of two extremes: It can either make you pride-filled or make you feel insecure and inferior. Comparisons become tremendously dangerous in a plethora of ways. One of the biggest comparison pitfalls occurs when a friend perceives and responds differently than we would. We think that our response is the only adequate one and that our friend's response is completely wrong. The end result is often rejection, control, and manipulation. Let's look at two examples: (1) when someone sins against your friend; and (2) when your friend sins.

Example 1: You are an assertive, outspoken, and zealous person, but your friend is a laid-back, soft-spoken, and patient person. Your friend reveals how a person deeply wounded her. You think she should confront the person about how she has been wounded. Your friend chooses to overlook the offense and move on. The Bible supports both responses as viable options in this type of circumstance (see Proverbs 19:11; Matthew 18:15; Galatians 6:1).

If you are not careful, you might get angry because your friend didn't respond the way you would have. You may even reject her or give her the silent treatment, withholding your love until she responds the way you want. You may talk down to her or talk bad about the person who hurt her in an attempt to manipulate your friend. When you react in such unhealthy ways, not only do you make your friend question her decision but you also breed mistrust in the genuineness of your love and friendship. She may begin to feel that unless she does things your way, she will not be accepted as your friend. This performance-based friendship is toxic. Certainly, you can offer advice based on the Word of God, but be careful of your response when a friend chooses another route, especially if it is also biblical. If her response is not biblical, then you can share in love what the Bible says about the matter.

Open your Bible and read 1 Corinthians 13:5. What does this verse say about being demanding?

> [Love] does not demand its own way. — 1 Corinthians 13:5, NLT

Example 2 (using the same two people): Your friend has sinned against God, and the results have been tremendously damaging. You counsel your friend to confess her sin to God, repent of it, and move on from that sin, knowing that God has forgiven her. Your friend is working through that process, but it is taking some time for her to stop punishing herself for her bad decision. While you may be able to quickly forgive yourself, your friend may need more time. If you respond with impatience and pressure, your friend may begin to feel insecure and inadequate because she can't seem to "get it together" as quickly as you can. She may also think that you can't be trusted to hang in there with her while she works through this issue. As a friend, you need to demonstrate patience and a commitment to be there with her as she works through things, no matter how long it takes.

In both of these examples, something else needs to be considered: How your friend chooses to handle situations may be God's way of showing you a different way to deal with some issues in your own life.

God takes each of His children along paths that are tailor-made for them. If you measure another's actions only against your own, you may never learn new, healthier ways to live. But if you appreciate another's path and look at it as an opportunity for you to grow, there will be no haughtiness on your part and no feelings of inadequacy on hers. Remember, friendship is about connecting with others and helping them (and you) become holy. Your differences may be the means for you to grow in a particular area of your life. Instead of comparing yourself to others, seek to learn from others! The friendship will definitely be more freeing and fulfilling.

Wrapping It Up

When a friendship gets to this depth, the best way to avoid the dangers associated with your differences is to offer patience, understanding, and love, even if your friend doesn't do what you might think is best. Consideration, acceptance, and appreciation of your differences can help you both grow and learn how to respond to your own sin and to others who sin against you.

Apply It!

Seek Upwardly

Thank God for making you the way you are, knowing that there is purpose in all of it. Thank God for making your friends the way they are, knowing that there is purpose in your differences.

Seek Inwardly

Write this phrase from 1 Corinthians 13:5: "[Love] does not demand its own way." Confess the times in your life when you have tried to make people be like you, demanding they respond the way you would. Ask God to reveal any ways in which you have been demanding and to help you not demand your own way but instead be patient and understanding with others.

In your journal, write some differences you and your friends have.

Ask the Lord to reveal how you could learn from those differences. Ask Him to help you appreciate those differences rather than demand that your friends respond the same way you would.

Seek Outwardly
Take a minute to tell a friend about a characteristic in her that is different from you and how much you appreciate and have learned from her as a result of that difference. You may even want to take her name and make an acrostic of all the Christlike characteristics you see and appreciate in her.

Day 3: Heart Check: Craving Authentic Relationships

Pray, *Holy Spirit, be my Teacher. Give me understanding on how to put what I learn today into practice. In the name of Jesus I ask, amen.*

· · · · · · · · ·

I am notorious for my sense of smell. I am also diligent about spraying my perfume on my wrists. I have found these two aspects of who I am to be very compatible. You see, when something stinks, I yell, "Smell your wrists!" and immediately, all my girlfriends smash their wrists to their noses to avoid the dreadful smell I just inhaled.

Stop for a second. Take a deep breath. What do you smell? Do you need to smell your wrists?

Open your Bible and read Proverbs 27:9. What does it say about friendship?

> The heartfelt counsel of a friend is as sweet as perfume and incense. — Proverbs 27:9, NLT

This Scripture says that when we offer heartfelt advice to a friend, it is a sweet fragrance to her. Yet most of us struggle with asking for help or advice. We want to know it all. We don't want to need anything or anybody. Our culture would call it self-reliance or self-sufficiency. Scripture would call it pride.

The reality is that we all need help. In order for us to grow, we need the encouragement, wisdom, and support of those who deeply care about us and love us. As we begin to uncover places of deep hurt within us, friends will need the freedom to share with us what God is saying to them to help us. The key is our willingness to lay aside our pride and accept the heartfelt counsel of our friends; and not only just accept it but long for it, because God uses friendship to help make us holy.

Open your Bible and read Matthew 5:6. How does this Scripture relate to our friendships and their counsel?

> Blessed are those who hunger and thirst for righteousness, for they will be filled. — Matthew 5:6

If you have quick access to the Internet, go to www.blueletterbible.com and find out what the main words mean. Record in your journal what you find about these words.

To *hunger and thirst* means "to pine after; to toil for; to crave; to be famished for daily sustenance." The term *righteousness* means "rightly related to God and others," while *filled* means "to gorge oneself from a garden, a pasture, or a court."

When I read about being filled from a garden, pasture, or court, I wanted to know why those three specific locations were mentioned. Here's what the Spirit revealed to me in my search:

1. The Garden of Eden was where the Tree of Life was located. When we hunger and thirst after living as God would have us, rightly related to Him through obedience, it is as if we are in the Garden of Eden getting to eat from the Tree of Life: a life of deep fulfillment.
2. In John 10, believers are referred to as sheep under the care of the Good Shepherd (Jesus). In addition, Psalm 23 says that God leads us into green pastures and restores our souls. When we crave right living, the Shepherd will lead us to the people and places that will offer us the pastures of spiritual nourishment for our souls.
3. Psalm 84:10-12 says, "Better is one day in your courts than a thousand elsewhere; I would rather be a doorkeeper in the house of my God than dwell in the tents of the wicked. For the LORD God is a sun and shield; the LORD bestows favor

and honor; no good thing does he withhold from those whose walk is blameless. O LORD Almighty, blessed is the man who trusts in you." In the Old Testament, being in the courts of God was synonymous with being in God's presence. Thus, being right (declared righteous) with God allows us to enjoy His presence every day. In Him, we find protection, favor, blessings, and more. This is what Jesus promises to fill us with as we thirst and hunger to live right with Him and others.

Based on our findings, then, we could write this attitude as, "Happy and fortunate are those who crave living in right relationship with God and others, for when they do, they are stuffed with deep fulfillment, soul healing, and God's blessing and favor that come from living in His presence."

God is so gracious to give us friends who care enough about us to counsel us on how to be rightly related to God and others. Not too long ago, my daughter was struggling with an issue in her life. She shared it with a friend, who said, "Let me take some time to pray about it and then I will share with you what God says for me to tell you." I was so impressed. When that friend came back and spoke some truths to our daughter — some uplifting and encouraging, and some challenging and hard — my daughter was able to receive it all because she knew this was a true friend who cared enough to carefully ask the Father what to say. That friend's words were sweet, like a comforting, familiar fragrance.

Open your Bible and read 2 Corinthians 2:15. How does this verse relate to our study today?

> For we are to God the aroma of Christ among those who are being saved and those who are perishing. — 2 Corinthians 2:15

When I was growing up, my home always smelled like one of two things: either very clean, because my mother kept an extremely clean home; or like a yummy, warm pound cake, because she baked one on a weekly basis. To this day, I feel a tranquil, consoling peace when I smell fresh-baked goods. Second Corinthians 2:15 says that whether we receive Christlike counsel or give it to another, it is a sweet-smelling fragrance that feels right at home and pleases the receiver.

Wrapping It Up

When you develop a deep desire, or craving, to live in right relationship with God and others, you will eat your fill of love, forgiveness, peace, mercy, grace, and more. God will give you friends who will counsel you on how to live in a way that pleases God as you reveal more and more of your life with them. As you receive their heartfelt counsel, it will be like a sweet, peaceful, and comforting fragrance to you. When you offer this same kind of counsel to another, you become the fragrance of Christ that is sweet and pleasing to your Father.

Apply It!

Seek Upwardly

Consider fasting from food (not water) for all or a portion of the day. Every time your stomach growls and craves food, say to your Father, "More than I crave food, I crave to live right before You and right with others. Show me how to do that, Lord. In Your name I ask, amen."

Draw a fork and then write this beatitude (Matthew 5:6) in your journal to remind you of the promise offered when you crave to be right with God and others. Record what the Lord reveals to you as you meditate on this verse.

Seek Inwardly

Write Proverbs 27:9 in your journal and ask God to help you be open to your friends' counsel. Ask Him to guard you from pride and to accept the counsel of your friends as it aligns to His Word. Thank God for the gift of friends who will give you godly counsel. Thank your friends for that as well.

Seek Outwardly
Write out 2 Corinthians 2:15 in your journal and ask the Holy Spirit to remind you to offer His counsel to others so you can be the fragrance of Christ. Spray a little of your perfume on your wrist and smell it often to remind you throughout the day about what you learned.

Day 4: No Room for Envy

Pray, *Holy Spirit, be my Teacher. Give me understanding on how to put what I learn today into practice. In the name of Jesus I ask, amen.*

. . . .

Picture this in your mind: There is a guy who falls in love with a beautiful woman. She is pregnant, very pregnant. They have to go home for a family reunion, and on the long trip back, she goes into labor. He begins to search everywhere for a place for his wife to have their child, but there is just no place in sight. How do you think this guy feels?

The reality is that this story comes straight out of the Bible. It is the account of Mary and Joseph and the birth of Jesus. Joseph must have felt helpless, alone, afraid, and hopeless. I believe that many people in our world today feel exactly the same way because they can find no safe place in friendship with another.

If we want to be a good friend, we must make room in our lives for friendships. We must also make room for the unveiling of ourselves to each other. As we do this, however, we must make no room in our friendships for envy. Envy is feeling resentful or discontent because of someone else's successes, possessions, or skills.

When our relationships get to a place of full disclosure, we can begin to compare our journey with our friends' journeys. If left unchecked, envy can creep in because others seem to be moving through their struggles faster than we are.

How slick and deceiving of the Enemy to sneak in and try to mess with our thoughts! The very thing we have wanted all along for our friends is healing and wholeness. They have finally opened up and are making progress, but instead of celebrating what God is doing, we become envious! All of the joy we anticipated for our friends' healing and freedom has been sucked from us in a pit of resentment and discontent. Envy can sabotage a friendship.

God warns us about envy. Open your Bible and read James 3:16. What does this verse tell us about envy?

> For where you have envy and selfish ambition, there you find disorder and every evil practice. — James 3:16

The word for "disorder" actually means "instability; a state of disorder, disturbance, confusion." When you become envious, your thinking becomes unstable and confused, and as a result, you begin acting in all kinds of horrible and hateful ways. Envy can consume and control you if you do not guard yourself from its trap. While you might think that you would never hurt your dear friend, envy has destroyed many friendships.

In 1 Samuel 16, the Bible tells us that King Saul was impressed by a young shepherd-warrior named David. Scripture tells us that Saul grew to love David very much. He even made David his armor-bearer, a role that required great trust of the king. You would think nothing would have come between them. But over time, David began getting more attention from the ladies.

First Samuel 18:6-9 says,

> When the men were returning home after David had killed the Philistine, the women came out from all the towns of Israel to meet King Saul with singing and dancing, with joyful songs and with tambourines and lutes. As they danced, they sang:
>
> "Saul has slain his thousands,
>   and David his tens of thousands."
>
> Saul was very angry; this refrain galled him. "They have credited David with tens of thousands," he thought, "but me with only thousands. What more can he get but the kingdom?" And from that time on Saul kept a jealous eye on David. — 1 Samuel 18:6-9

Once friends who loved each other very much, Saul and David saw envy wreak havoc on their friendship.

The best way to guard yourself against becoming envious of your friends' spiritual growth is to remember that you all are on different pathways that are totally unique from each other. Comparisons would be unfair because the paths are so different. Your journey with God is your personal journey designed to perfect you and make you whole. Whether your journey is longer or more painful than others' is irrelevant. The point is that you are on the journey and are promised that your healing will come. To this end you keep your focus, and to this end you forge ahead no matter how long it takes or how hard the road becomes. When you keep this right perspective about your journey, you can rejoice at the success and progress of your friends. This perspective also gives you hope and courage to press on in your own journey as you see your friends making progress.

The movie *Beaches* chronicles the lives of two women as they mature, succeed, fail, and grow together and apart. At various points in the movie, Hillary and CC are so envious of each other that their jealousy threatens to tear apart the friendship. Both characters finally realize that they are two very different people, with their own paths and their own pursuits. This realization allows them to like themselves and to embrace their differences, and the friendship is transformed into a partnership that helps the other grow into a better person. Because they eventually made no room for envy, they found a safe haven in each other.

Wrapping It Up

When your friends begin to find healing, forgiveness, and freedom from their past sins and wounds, be a safe place for them. Rejoice with them, knowing that God used you to help encourage them on their journey. Guard against envy by remembering that you are on your own journey and that others will one day rejoice with you as well.

Apply It!

Seek Upwardly

Take a look at your journey with Jesus. Look at where you were and where you are now. Thank God for the growth and healing He has given you. Thank Him for being with you during the journey and for giving you friends who encourage you. Thank Him for using every bad situation for your good. Tell Him you trust Him to take you through the necessary process to make you all that He wants you to be.

Seek Inwardly

In your journal, draw a face and color it green. Next to it, draw a flower growing out of green grass. Underneath, write this question: "Will you be green with envy or green with growth?" Then write James 3:16 in your journal. Ask the Lord to help you not become envious of your friends but rather to be grateful and happy that you are growing and working through your sins and wounds together.

Seek Outwardly

Take some time to rejoice with a friend over some success she has found in her life as she walks with God. If you have seen someone overcome some area of unforgiveness or sinful addiction, make it a point to tell her how proud God is of her and how happy you are for her. Don't assume she knows how you feel. Your words may be just what she needs to keep pressing on toward her freedom.

Day 5: A Promise to Be Made

Pray, *Holy Spirit, be my Teacher. Give me understanding on how to put what I learn today into practice. In the name of Jesus I ask, amen.*

• • • • • • • • •

The last two weeks have given attention to the level of friendship called The Cover-Up. I pray that God has brought safe friends into your life with whom you feel comfortable and able to open and unveil yourself. I pray that you are pushing through your fears and removing your masks and that your friends are doing the same. During this time we learned the importance of being AVAILABLE through CONSISTENT ENCOUNTERS and being teachable so we can learn from each other as we unveil hurtful places. This takes time, and making yourself open to meet and talk is so valuable in the process of healing.

Once you and a friend discover that you are committed to sharing your hearts, it is imperative that you both are ACCEPTING of one another and that you treat each other with CONSIDERATE ACCEPTANCE. Considering one another's past, upbringing, temptations, and wounds yields much compassion, acceptance, and grace for the other. We must protect ourselves from comparison and envy and seek the counsel of God and His Word to live in right relationship with Him and others. We must crave that kind of living so much that we would open ourselves up to godly advice from our friends and learn to accept the truth as they remind us what God says about us.

You can guard against comparison and envy in your relationships by making a commitment to God about how you will respond to others when they begin to reveal deep places within.

May I suggest we all make this commitment as we continue to walk through the removing of our Cover-Ups in friendship?

"I will be present with my friends through the hard times."

This means that you will commit to hang in there with a friend as she works through some difficult things in her life. A beautiful verse in Proverbs says, "A friend loves at all times, and a brother is born for adversity" (17:17). A true friend will love you no matter what you tell her, no matter what you've been through, and no matter what mistakes you have made. A true friend will not run when your life gets tough but rather will realize that she has the unique opportunity to be your friend during this difficult season of your life.

How many times have we seen so-called friends hang around someone until tragedy, accusation, or negative situations occur? Suddenly those friends are nowhere to be found. They run away in shock over what has been revealed or don't want their names to be tarnished or their reputations tainted. This leaves the person feeling alone and rejected. Wounded, she crawls deeper into her cave of shame. Most of the time, people like this resolve never to come back out again.

Proverbs 17:17 says that when a friend is going through adverse circumstances or struggles, a true friend says, "Yes! I was born for this!" and seizes the moment to step in and be there through thick and thin, never leaving her friend's side.

Now think about this: God has made this same commitment to you: **"I will always be present with you through the hard times."**

In Matthew 28:20, God promised that He would never leave you. No matter what you are going through, God's presence will never leave. He is always with you. What a comfort to know that though others may leave you and forsake you in your greatest hour of need, your Father God will not. When you commit to do this for your friend, you partner with the Lord in what He is doing in the life of your friend and follow in His footsteps as His disciple by doing just what He did.

Wrapping It Up

As your week concludes, ask the Holy Spirit to help you put into practice what you learned; ask in the name of Jesus.

Apply It!

Seek Upwardly

Write this friendship commitment in your journal and refer to it today and in the days to come. Ask God to help you be present when your friends are having tough times.

Seek Inwardly

Take some time to write in your journal about what stuck out to you as God revealed Himself to you this week. Write down how this truth has affected your relational views of God and others, as well as how it will change the way you live in relationship with God and others.

Seek Outwardly

Become more accepting of your friends when they share a difficult place in their lives, as you consider all they have gone through. Appreciate your differences and try to understand them. Crave being right with God and others so that your relationships are fulfilling. Guard against envy and instead celebrate each of your unique journeys. And by all means, rise to the occasion when your friends need you on their side.

week 5

the blinders (part 1)

Day 1: Attached

Pray, *Holy Spirit, be my Teacher. Give me understanding on how to put what I learn today into practice. In the name of Jesus I ask, amen.*

· · · · · · · · ·

If you have ever watched horses race, you have seen the blinders placed upon their eyes. The blinders are there to keep the horse focused on what is before her and to keep out the distractions that could detour her from her goal. (Too bad I can't wear blinders around hot dough-nut shops! I get drawn in every time!)

Over time, certain friends may show that they truly care about you and your wholeness. They have allowed you to unveil your sin and shame and have been there to encourage you in the healing process. From this an opportunity may surface. They may have the privilege of helping you remove the blind spots in your life: those areas that are potentially hazardous and that you don't see. But even greater than helping you remove the blind spots is the placing of blinders on your eyes so you can remain focused on becoming all that God wants you to become. That's why this next level of friendship is called **The Blinders**. Each of you helps the other stay focused on what is important and not be distracted by the millions of diversions that tend to lure us away. This area of closeness in the relationship must be reciprocated. Both of you must be given the privilege to participate in the other's wholeness and freedom.

If this removing of blind spots and replacing with blinders is going to be a life-giving process, the friendship will require that you be **ATTACHED** in a healthy way. What I mean by this is demonstrating "faithful support for a cause"—the cause being helping each other grow into Christlikeness. Each friend wants what is best for the other and is committed to helping her achieve it. Such a friend is even willing to set herself aside for a while to see a friend fulfill the purpose for which she was created.

With this privilege also comes a responsibility. If friends choose to move to this deeper progression in the friendship, they each must offer a **CONTRIBUTING DEVOTION** to one another. They must be devoted to helping their friend, willing to play whatever part necessary to see a friend through. This deeper level of friendship involves wholehearted devotion to the good of the other, giving time, energy, creativity, and attentiveness. One of the greatest ways to bring yourself delight and happiness is to contribute to the well-being of your friends. Seeking the good of the other is the central aim of every good friendship.

There is no one more devoted to you than Jesus. One of His most beautiful and endearing qualities is His faithfulness. He promises to never leave us. He knows us better than we know ourselves and is devoted to seeing us become all that He intended for us to be. Throughout the Bible, in story after story, God proves His faithfulness to His people.

Open your Bible and read Philippians 1:6. What does this say about God's commitment to us? Record your thoughts in your journal.

Being confident of this, that he who began a good work in you will carry it on to completion until the day of Christ Jesus.
—Philippians 1:6

God is completely devoted to your wholeness. He is faithful to you. He will complete the work of making you whole and holy. But He desires His followers to be faithful too.

Now read Psalm 18:25 in your Bible or read it here. What does this verse tell you about God's faithfulness?

> To the faithful you show yourself faithful, to the blameless you show yourself blameless. — Psalm 18:25

God is a faithful God who promises to complete everything He started in us. But He also wants us to be faithful to Him by being obedient to His Word. The question is, will you be faithful to Him and stick with Him through the process? Will you let Him and your close friends help you see and remove your blind spots while also placing some blinders on you?

Wrapping It Up

In order for you to become whole, you must allow faithful God and faithful friends to help you and support you, and your friends must allow you to do the same.

Apply It!

Seek Upwardly

Draw or trace your hands in your journal in a way that makes them overlapped and attached. Write a word of thanksgiving to God for His faithfulness to take you by the hand and lead you in completing the purposes for which you were created. Let these hands serve as a reminder of God's promise of contributing devotion to you.

Seek Inwardly

Record Philippians 1:6 in your journal and try to memorize it this week. Do some inward searching about how faithful you are to God and others: What holds you back? What can you do to show your devotion to God and others? Commit yourself to partnering with God as He completes His work in you.

Seek Outwardly

As the Lord leads you, make a card for a friend with your hands traced on it. Share with her that you are attaching yourself to her by faithfully supporting her in becoming all that God intends for her and that you are willing to help however the Lord and she would allow. Ask her to do the same for you. When your faithful God or your faithful friend reveals a blind spot to you or seeks to help you keep your focus, ask God to help you receive that advice or correction graciously. Ask God to make your heart ready for this help and to receive it with joy because of the growth that will take place as a result.

If there are those in your life who have already been a devoted friend, thank God for them and give them a word of thanks.

Day 2: Beware the Dangers of Discouragement

Pray, *Holy Spirit, be my Teacher. Give me understanding on how to put what I learn today into practice. In the name of Jesus I ask, amen.*

. . . .

There is nothing more disturbing than looking in your rearview mirrors and pulling into the adjacent lane, only to hear a driver slam on the brakes (and the horn!) because you didn't see the car in your blind spot!

Today we need to define a blind spot. A blind spot is an area in your life that does not bring honor or pleasure to God, but because it has been a part of your life for so long, you are unaware of it.

For example, let's imagine a girl named Catherine. God has standards for Catherine to live by, given for her protection and spelled out for her in His Word. One of those standards is to be morally pure, particularly saving herself sexually until she is married. Catherine has a deep need for unconditional love and acceptance, as well as a deep need for the security of knowing that she will never be abandoned. The need is so large in her life that she began to believe the only way to find love, acceptance, and security was to give herself sexually to a guy. One guy led to another guy and then to another.

Later on in life, Catherine repented of the way she had lived, purposed to live a life that would please God, and eventually married a godly man. She could look back on her life and see how far she had come from what she used to be, and she was encouraged with her improvement. There was just one problem: A constant conflict recurred in their marriage. Her husband accused her of being way too flirty with other men, but she always denied it. Her husband remained extremely frustrated with the situation. Not only was this affecting their marriage, but because Catherine was flirting with their married guy friends, the wives wanted nothing to do with them anymore. Yet Catherine couldn't understand what everyone's problem was.

Catherine had a blind spot, but she couldn't see it because she was focused on how much she had already grown instead of looking ahead at what God still desired for her. Her husband saw the gap between what she perceived as right behavior and what he knew as God's way for a holy woman to live.

At this point, Catherine had a choice. She could believe that her husband was just jealous, that he was paranoid, and that he was overly possessive and needed to get over it. Or she could believe that his heart toward her was good, that he desired her to be all that God created her to be, and that he loved her deeply and wanted to partner with her in becoming more like Jesus.

Everybody has blind spots; therefore, everyone needs people who care deeply enough to tell the other what those blind spots are. Might it be embarassing? Even humiliating? Painful? Discouraging? Yes. But necessary for growth into Christlikeness.

Oftentimes in my own life, I have experienced someone sharing with me a blind spot in my life. My first response was, "How dare she! Who does she think she is?" After I got through that initial selfish, void-of-God response, I realized I had given this person permission to point out my blind spots. I was also reminded that she loved me and had my best interests at heart, so I could trust what she said.

Catherine's husband in the story also had a choice to make. He could love her enough to press through his fears of hurting her, fears of her rejecting him, and fears of losing her love in order to confront her about this blind spot. Or he could resolve that she would never change and spend the rest of their lives resenting her actions that felt like betrayal to him.

Looking at this situation from the outside, it is easy to see that Catherine needs to listen to the loving concern of her husband and let him show her her blind spot as he presses through his fears and loves her enough to risk it. Sadly, many people never get to this place in their relationships, so they never grow.

What's even more saddening is that many times both parties in the friendship become increasingly discouraged. The word *discourage* means "without courage." When one of the people sees that there is no hope for this issue in the relationship to change, he or she develops a loss of courage to keep trying. When the other goes on living with the blind spot and never reaches the free and fulfilling life she thought she would have in a relationship with Jesus, she, too, develops a lack of courage to keep on pressing in to God. Blind spots can cause a cycle that spirals downward until both people in the relationship want out.

Just recently I heard a woman speak these discouraging words to another: "People don't change, and you will never change." Let me tell you, friends, that is a lie, because it is in direct conflict with God's Word.

Open your Bible and read 2 Corinthians 3:18. What does this verse tell us about our capacity to change and become more like Christ?

And we, who with unveiled faces all reflect the Lord's glory, are being transformed into his likeness with ever-increasing glory, which comes from the Lord, who is the Spirit. — 2 Corinthians 3:18

When we become a Christian, God begins to change us from the inside out, becoming more like Him in His character. The only people who don't change are those who refuse to allow God to change them. All people can change. People are not doomed to a life of discouragement, depression, and defeat. God offers us life, wholeness, and real living as we walk with Him and grow into His likeness.

Wrapping It Up

Guard against the dangers of discouragement by allowing close, trusted friends to share with you the blind spots they see in your life that need to be called out. Be willing to let God change that area in your life. Press through your own fears of rejection and love others enough to lovingly show them their blind spots.

Apply It!

Seek Upwardly

Write 2 Corinthians 3:18 in your journal. Tell God that you want to be all He created you to be and are willing to let Him reveal your blind spots so you can become more like Him. As you go throughout your day, every time you open a door, say to the Father, "I am opening myself up to You."

Seek Inwardly

Ask the Lord to give you a receptive heart when He or your friend shows you a blind spot in your life. Ask Him to help you not be defensive or offended. Also ask the Lord to help you lovingly confront your friends about their blind spots in a way that is life-giving and beneficial.

Seek Outwardly

Ask the Lord to reveal to you which friends should have permission to show you your blind spots. Then humbly ask them to do just that. Hopefully they will ask you to do the same. If not, move forward, trusting God's prompting for you to do this, knowing that He has a plan. If you already have a person in your life who does this, thank her for loving you enough to press through her own fears and show you your blind spots. Tell her that you love and appreciate her.

Day 3: Heart Check: Merciful

Pray, *Holy Spirit, be my Teacher. Give me understanding on how to put what I learn today into practice. In the name of Jesus I ask, amen.*

. . . .

I once had someone share with me a blind spot in my life. Again, after I went through the process of reminding myself that the person loved me and was helping me, I came to realize that what she had revealed to me was true. I asked God to remind me every time I acted in that particular way so I could correct this blind spot in my life. It has taken a long time for me to grow in this area, and I still struggle with it today. The friend who first shared this blind spot with me got very upset when I didn't automatically change and stop my behavior altogether. This friend assumed that if she made me aware of this problem, I would fix it immediately. When change didn't happen on her timetable, she began to withhold her love. She showed disgust with me when I messed up and became impatient with me about other flaws in my life.

If we are going to move into close relationships with others in The Blinders level of friendship, we must be patient and merciful as they work through their blind spots. The word *mercy* has best been described as "not giving others what they deserve." God has been so merciful to me. As a sinner, I deserved eternal separation for my sin, but God didn't give me what I deserved; rather, He sent His only Son to take the punishment for my sin so that my relationship with Him could be restored. If God offered you and me such great mercy, how dare we not give that same mercy to others? You may think that a friend deserves to be chastised, pushed, or prodded to fix a problem, but what she needs from you is mercy.

Open your Bible and read Matthew 5:7. What does this verse tell you about mercy?

Blessed are the merciful, for they will be shown mercy. — Matthew 5:7

Here's how we might write this verse based on what we have learned about mercy: "Happy and fortunate are those who don't give others what they deserve; otherwise, when they themselves need mercy, others will not give it." This principle sounds a lot like Matthew 7:12, a verse that has commonly been called The Golden Rule: "So in everything, do to others what you would have them do to you." In other words, if you want to be shown mercy, then you best be showing mercy!

We live in a "no mercy" society. Even Christians, those who call themselves followers of Jesus Christ and commit to walk as He walked, sometimes take pride in saying, "I have no mercy. I show no mercy. It's just who I am." This runs counter to God's own character.

Read Micah 6:8 in your Bible or read it here. What does this verse tell us about mercy?

> He has showed you, O man, what is good. And what does the LORD require of you? To act justly and to love mercy and to walk humbly with your God. — Micah 6:8

God says that He not only wants us to be merciful, but He also wants us to *love* being merciful! God wants us to wake up each morning and say, "I can't wait to show someone mercy! I just love it!" It means that when a person cuts you off in traffic or makes you late because he or she is driving so slow, you are to get excited and exclaim, "Yeah! I get to show you mercy! I just love it!"

Now if God challenges us to actually *love* showing mercy to a stranger, how much more is it necessary for us to offer it to our closest friends?

One of the many times that my children disobeyed me, the Lord spoke to me and told me to teach them the difference between grace and mercy — grace being "giving to someone what they do not deserve," and mercy being "not giving them what they do deserve." So I baked some cookies and called my disobedient children into the kitchen. I told them, "Because of your disobedience, you deserve a spanking. Today you are just going to get warned and be given the opportunity to obey me and do what I asked you to do. This is mercy: not giving you what you deserve. And while you don't deserve a chocolate chip cookie, I'm going to give you one anyway. This is grace: giving you what you do not deserve."

I am sure my children would have wanted me to always respond in that manner with them, but the reality is, I have not. Maybe in our friendships we just need to offer the kind of mercy we want to be given and serve each other a whole lot of warm and sweet grace . . . with a glass of milk!

Wrapping It Up
We will help our friends grow as we show them their blind spots and then offer mercy instead of judgment and impatience. As they work to root out their ungodly behavior and replace it with the new, offer them the mercy that you have been so graciously given.

Apply It!
Seek Upwardly
Draw a chocolate chip cookie in your journal. Write the definition of mercy and grace beside it. Also write the beatitude (Matthew 5:7). Thank God for His great mercy to you and ask Him to help you give it away to others.

Seek Inwardly
Ask the Holy Spirit to help you live a life in which you love to show mercy to those around you. Look for ways to show mercy. Be patient with your friends who are working through issues in their lives. Don't chide them or get angry with them when they don't change as fast as you want them to. Show mercy in the way that you would want it shown to you.

Seek Outwardly

Think of all the times when you have needed mercy. Thank the people in your life who have shown you the Father's mercy by the way they have offered it to you. Maybe you could bake them some cookies and tell them the story about mercy and grace. What a great way to say thank you!

Day 4: No Room for Judgment

Pray, *Holy Spirit, be my Teacher. Give me understanding on how to put what I learn today into practice. In the name of Jesus I ask, amen.*

. . . .

The book of John contains a valuable story about Jesus:

> At dawn he appeared again in the temple courts, where all the people gathered around him, and he sat down to teach them. The teachers of the law and the Pharisees brought in a woman caught in adultery. They made her stand before the group and said to Jesus, "Teacher, this woman was caught in the act of adultery. In the Law Moses commanded us to stone such women. Now what do you say?" They were using this question as a trap, in order to have a basis for accusing him.
>
> But Jesus bent down and started to write on the ground with his finger. When they kept on questioning him, he straightened up and said to them, "If any one of you is without sin, let him be the first to throw a stone at her." Again he stooped down and wrote on the ground.
>
> At this, those who heard began to go away one at a time, the older ones first, until only Jesus was left, with the woman still standing there. Jesus straightened up and asked her, "Woman, where are they? Has no one condemned you?"
>
> "No one, sir," she said.
>
> "Then neither do I condemn you," Jesus declared. "Go now and leave your life of sin." — John 8:2-11

Was Jesus saying that since everyone sins, sin doesn't matter? Not at all. What Jesus was saying is that there is no room for judgment that leads to condemnation because we have all sinned and we all stand in need of forgiveness. Who are you to stand in the seat of judgment over someone's sin when you yourself sin?

Many people have taken out of context the Scriptures that talk about not judging others. These people say that as Christians we are not supposed to judge each other. As a result, when someone brings a blind spot to their attention, they angrily throw out, "You don't have a right to judge me!"

The truth is that the Bible uses many different words for the English word *judge*. Sometimes the Bible uses the word *krino*, which means "to pronounce a verdict without any involvement." In Matthew 7:1-2, Jesus told His disciples (and us) not to pronounce a verdict on others: "Do not judge (*krino*), or you too will be judged. For in the same way you judge (*krino*) others, you will be judged, and with the measure you use, it will be measured to you."

Open your Bible and read Matthew 7:1-2. If you evaluated how you judge people, would you want that kind of judgment made over you?

> Do not judge, or you too will be judged. For in the same way you judge others, you will be judged, and with the measure you use, it will be measured to you. — Matthew 7:1-2

However, the Bible uses two other words for *judge*. The first is *anakrino*, which means "to investigate, interrogate, and examine in order to give an estimate of." The second usage is *diakrino*, which means "to reason; to distinguish."

Did you notice the difference between pronouncing judgment and the spiritual gift of discernment? To discern is to ask questions. To judge is to form an opinion without asking questions. Discernment discovers roots of the bad fruit with a heart to help. Judgment jumps to conclusions and then broadcasts it to others without offering any help. A person of discernment takes a long hard look at herself first. A person of judgment is consumed with others' sin and avoids her own. Discernment accepts and offers a helping hand. Judgment cannot separate the sin from the sinner and thus rejects both.

So which one are you? A judge or a discerner? Which have you seen more in your lifetime?

To truly grow into Christlikeness, we must stop judging and start discerning. As a matter of fact, when you look at the places in the Bible that talk about discernment, you'll notice that the Scripture always starts with self-evaluation first (see Matthew 7:3). So if we really want to obey the Bible, we must first ask the Lord to show us our own blind spots and then begin to walk with God and find transformation and healing in those areas. The change in our lives will result in others seeing their own need for change, and then we can help them. That's the way God intended the process to work.

Wrapping It Up

When helping one another recognize and root out blind spots, there is no room for judgment—only discernment.

Apply It!

Seek Upwardly

Draw a line in your journal that separates the page into two sections. In one section write characteristics of judgment, and in the second section write characteristics of discernment. Under this, write out Matthew 7:1. Thank God that He is the only judge. Confess times when you have taken His place and judged others.

Seek Inwardly

Ask God to reveal to you the beam in your own eye before you try to get the speck out of your friend's eye (see Matthew 7:3). Ask Him to show you how to best come alongside your friend to help her with her blind spots.

Seek Outwardly

Ask God to reveal people you need to ask forgiveness from for being a judge over their lives. Commit to being only a helpful discerner for them as you assist each other in getting rid of blind spots in your lives.

Day 5: A Promise to Be Made

Pray, *Holy Spirit, be my Teacher. Give me understanding on how to put what I learn today into practice. In the name of Jesus I ask, amen.*

. . . .

It has been my prayer throughout this week that you have seen that God is your closest friend. No one could ever be as faithfully committed to your wholeness than He. My prayer is that you have seen that He is eternally ATTACHED to you and offers you His CONTRIBUTING DEVOTION. I pray that you have determined to be faithful to Him through obedience and to be grateful enough for His mercy that you love giving it away. This builds such a closeness between you and God that it makes living like Him exciting. I also pray that you have begun to see the importance of being a friend who is healthily attached and merciful to others in friendship.

This week we have spent a lot of time on what we do not need to give others, namely discouragement and judgment. What we *do* need to offer others is hope. Hope is not a wish that is usually coupled with doubt, such as "I wish I would win a million dollars! I probably won't get it, but I sure do wish for it!" Hope as defined in the Bible is far from that definition. Hope as the Bible defines it is "a confident expectancy that God will do what He says He will do." Therefore, when God says He is faithful to complete the good work that He began in you (see Philippians 1:6), you can bet your bottom dollar that He will do it.

So instead of focusing on the areas in your lives that need to be changed, focus on the God who says that nothing is too hard for Him. He is faithful to change you if you will surrender to Him. Put on your blinders and place them on your friends as well. Give them some God-defined hope.

May I suggest we all make this commitment as we seek to remove blind spots and place Blinders on our friendships?

"I will put hope before my friends."

This means you will commit not to focus on your friend's blind spots but rather to put the focus on the great things that God promises to do. In a world of such hopelessness, one of the greatest gifts you can give to breathe life into your friends is to offer them hope, a confidence to expect God to do great things in and through them as they surrender themselves to His lordship in their lives.

Another part of this commitment means putting aside all judgment and committing to ask God for discernment first in your own life and then in your friend's life in an effort to help her. And with that is an even deeper commitment to join your friends and help them as they work through their blind spots.

The beauty in this commitment is that God has also made it to you: **"I have and will continue to put hope before you."**

Read 1 Thessalonians 5:24 in your Bible. How does this verse apply to God's work in your life?

> The one who calls you is faithful and he will do it. — 1 Thessalonians 5:24

God has proven Himself trustworthy. He will do whatever it takes to see that we become what He originally designed us to be. He proved that by dying for us, and He continues to prove it by His presence with us. While we remain hopeful and merciful, we can rely on His promise to be faithful to do what He set out to do: make us holy.

When you choose to offer hope to your friend, you are partnering with the Lord as He is doing the same thing! How awesome to think that God would grant us the privilege and responsibility to follow His example.

Wrapping It Up

As you close this week, ask the Holy Spirit to help you to put into practice what you learned; ask in the name of Jesus.

Apply It!

Seek Upwardly

Write this friendship commitment in your journal and refer to it today and in the days to come. Ask God to help you offer hope to others.

Seek Inwardly

Take some time to write in your journal about what stuck out to you as God revealed Himself to you this week. Write down how this truth has affected your relational views of God and others, as well as how it will change the way you live in relationship with God and others.

Seek Outwardly

Ask God to help you show faithful support to your close friends as they walk through the process of recognizing blind spots and placing on new blinders. Press through your fears as you share their blind spots and allow your friends to show you your blind spots to protect the friendships from discouragement and destruction. Offer mercy, not judgment, and always put hope before them. These actions will breathe life into your friends and your friendships.

week 6

the blinders (part 2)

Day 1: Accountable

Pray, *Holy Spirit, be my Teacher. Give me understanding on how to put what I learn today into practice. In the name of Jesus I ask, amen.*

· · · · · · · · ·

Read each of the following four scenarios and think about how you might respond.

Scenario 1: You've developed a wonderful friendship with someone. You've shared some very personal parts of your life with her and have sacrificially given to your best ability in support of her and your friendship with her. Out of nowhere, she steps away from the friendship with no explanation. When you ask for some clarification as to what happened, she refuses to answer. How do you feel?

Scenario 2: You've developed a wonderful friendship with someone. You've shared some very personal parts of your life with her, namely that you have a hard time trusting others because of wounds from your past. She has shared with you that she struggles with overcommitting. When she cancels an important event with you that has been on the calendar for a long while and chooses a much less important event to participate in, you ask her to explain why she made the choice. Instead of owning her bad choice and humbling herself, becoming teachable and learning from it, she turns the tables on you and tells you it is all because of your lack of trust that you are even asking and she doesn't see her need to change at all. How does that make you feel?

Scenario 3: You have developed a very special relationship with a person. You have observed an area of compromise in her life that if not addressed has the potential for devastation. To keep the friendship intact, you've chosen not to say something, and now that person is far from God and headed for major destruction. How do you feel?

Scenario 4: You basically have no relationship with a certain person. She has made no investments in you, has little to no knowledge of you, and has no understanding of your heart. She rings your doorbell, comes into your home for the first time, and proceeds to tell you what you've done wrong and what things she thinks you need to change in your life. How would that make you feel? How would you want to respond?

Have you ever heard the phrase "caught red-handed" or "caught with your hand in the cookie jar"? I heard them growing up, and most of the time when I was caught doing something I was not supposed to, I was asked to explain my knuckleheaded choices!

This week we will talk about the need to be **ACCOUNTABLE** in relationships. Being held accountable can be one of the most transformational things that ever happens to you, or it can be one of the most tragic. The word literally means "to give an answer or explanation to." The purpose of good and healthy accountability is transformation of your character, but unfortunately, many people don't know what it requires. That ignorance can cause a lot of wounds to people. Accountability in friendship takes place in one of two ways: when one has revealed something deep within herself with which she needs help, or when someone feels led to confront another about a sinful area. Yet no matter what the circumstance for the accountability, the giver must develop **COURAGEOUS ENCOURAGEMENT.**

Courageous encouragement may sound redundant, but in reality it is a great description. The person who holds another accountable must have great courage. She must also be able to give encouragement so her friend is strong enough to face the difficult places in her life and grow. God gives us these friends to help us become more authentically who we were made to be. Our friends help us find freedom from our fears, anxieties, past, and flaws. The best gift a friend can give is to partner with us to help us overcome obstacles that keep us from living the life God has for us. Many times, this encouragement comes through our words.

Open your Bible and read Ephesians 4:29. What does this verse say about the words we use with others?

> Do not let any unwholesome talk come out of your mouths, but only what is helpful for building others up according to their needs, that it may benefit those who listen. — Ephesians 4:29

Or as my husband says, "You never have to apologize for an unkind word never spoken."

We need good friends who will speak encouraging words into our lives. This is another vital piece to the puzzle of connection.

Holding us in loving accountability takes a lot of courage. It is a risky and scary thing to ask a friend to "give an answer or explanation" about her behavior or attitudes. Yet the most loving thing we can do is push through the fear and love others enough not to leave them living a life that is less than the life God has for them.

While friends who hold us accountable are an invaluable tool to help us grow, we are ultimately accountable to God for our lives. He holds us accountable by His Word. He gave us Scripture as our standard for living, not because He is mean and doesn't want us to have things or have fun. Rather, God uses His Word as protective boundaries. When they were young, I let my children go out and play in the yard, but I commanded that they not go out into the street. I was not withholding something good from them; I was protecting them from something bad. This is the heart of the Father toward us. He knows us better than we know ourselves and knows the best way for us to find real happiness and fulfillment in our lives. This is His purpose for His commands in Scripture. And Scripture is full of God offering us courage to live in obedience and trust in His faithfulness.

God holds us accountable not only *by* His Word but also *to* His Word. God gives us His Word as our boundary markers of protection, but He also reminds us that we will one day give an answer regarding how well we walked in obedience to them. It's not enough just to know God's Word. Obedience must follow.

We will also have to give an answer for how well we used our words to encourage others through loving accountability. Read Matthew 12:36-37 in your Bible or read it here. Summarize it in your journal.

> But I tell you that men will have to give account on the day of judgment for every careless word they have spoken. For by your words you will be acquitted, and by your words you will be condemned. — Matthew 12:36-37

One reason accountability has gone wrong is because people have misused and abused the Scriptures to manipulate and control others. We will be held accountable for the way we treat others with our words. We are in this thing together. We had better get courageous and give each other the encouragement we need!

Wrapping It Up

As we understand God's purposes in accountability, we can grow personally as we learn to stand accountable to God's Word. We can also help our friends grow when we offer accountability in a way that produces transformation in their hearts and lives.

Apply It!

Seek Upwardly

Take a moment to thank God for His Word, the standard by which you align your life. Thank Him that He didn't tell you to be holy and then leave you to figure it out. Rather, He gave you His own words to explain what holiness looks like. Write Him a note of thanks in your journal.

Seek Inwardly

Write Ephesians 4:29 in your journal and begin to memorize the verse this week. Talk with God about your words: Are they wholesome or not? What needs to change about your words so that they please Him? Ask God to reveal to you areas where you may need to be held accountable and then ask Him to show you the right friend to ask for accountability. Then press through your fears, take off your mask, and ask for help.

Seek Outwardly

When people give you the permission to share a blind spot you see in their lives, ask God to reveal to you how to courageously edify them in a way that helps them grow. Think of a friend who is aware of a blind spot in her life. Ask God to give you one Scripture verse to offer or the words to say to encourage her. Then push through your fears and offer those words to her, trusting that God will use them in her life.

Day 2: Beware the Dangers of Domination

Pray, *Holy Spirit, be my Teacher. Give me understanding on how to put what I learn today into practice. In the name of Jesus I ask, amen.*

. . . .

Today, revisit the four scenarios that were introduced to you yesterday. Go back and read them again on page 115. Let's see what God says about them.

Scenario 1: Annihilation. As you journey through friendships, you will find that some people have no problem holding others accountable; they just don't want to be held accountable themselves. To avoid their own accountability, they will constantly make accusations in an effort to blame you so that they never have to change. Or they will end the friendship abruptly because they have become too close and they are afraid their weaknesses will be exposed.

There is a similar story in the Bible. It centers around two brothers, Cain and Abel. Abel made a sacrifice that was pleasing to God while Cain did not. Cain ended up killing Abel. Why? Because instead of seeing Abel as a friend who could have helped him better understand why his sacrifice was not acceptable and learning from him, Cain saw Abel as a threat. Cain saw Abel as the one who beat him or was better than him, and to avoid facing his own weaknesses, Cain annihilated the very one who could have potentially helped him grow.

Open your Bible and read Proverbs 12:1. What does this verse say about correction?

Whoever loves discipline loves knowledge, but he who hates correction is stupid. — Proverbs 12:1

This verse says that it is foolish to hate correction; it is wise to love it. Unfortunately, rather than becoming vulnerable as a result of others' correction, most people would rather destroy someone else, much like Cain killed Abel.

Scenario 2: Arrogance. In some friendships, one friend will use a vulnerability that was disclosed by a friend to avoid any accountability on her part. If you seek to hold her accountable and she can somehow turn the tables to focus on a flaw in you, then she can remain the same and you will have to be the one who changes. If the friend can make you feel that the issue is really about your blind spots, sins, or flaws, then she won't have to look at the blind spots in her own life. Thus, her "perfect" view of herself can stay intact. We call this "passing the buck." It is arrogance, an overbearing pride, that keeps us from receiving when someone holds us accountable.

In 1 Samuel 20, King Saul was extremely concerned about David's popularity. Though David was more loyal than most, Saul felt so threatened by his right living that he tried to have David killed. Saul's son, Jonathan, was David's best friend. Jonathan approached his father, Saul, to hold him accountable for wanting to kill David. Saul got angry and proceeded to call Jonathan some horrible names. Jonathan said, "Why should he be put to death? What has he done?" Saul got so angry at being held accountable by his own son (because he knew his son was right) that instead of owning it and repenting, he actually threw a spear at his son to kill him, too! What lengths this guy went to out of his own pride and arrogance. He didn't want to be exposed and he didn't want to change, so he thought he could just blame his son for betrayal and destroy him. Romans 11:20 says, "Do not be arrogant." God is in control, and He can humble you if you will not humble yourself and listen to the counsel of close friends.

Scenario 3: Avoidance. Sometimes we see an area in a friend's life that has the potential to destroy her, but out of fear, we choose not to say anything. Then when the destruction occurs, we beat ourselves up with the guilt that had we said something, this may not have occurred. Usually we are unsure how she will receive the confrontation and fear losing the friendship. The fear of rejection and the fear of abandonment can so consume us that we will avoid the very things necessary to keep the friendship from growing stagnant.

Read Proverbs 3:27 in your Bible or read it here. How does this verse relate to friendship?

> Do not withhold good from those who deserve it, when it is in your power to act. — Proverbs 3:27

Proverbs 3:27 challenges us to not withhold good from those who need help when it is in our power to help them. Just as it is imperative to save your friend from walking in front of a speeding car, it is important to confront a friend and keep her from making a mistake that could cause her much heartache.

Scenario 4: Arrogation. When accountability is offered before being welcomed, wounds are inflicted and can rarely be healed. In this instance, a person assumed a role that was never theirs to take, a role reserved only for a close friend. When you arrogate, or assume, a depth in friendship that you have not earned, you can be assured a fatal outcome.

Read Proverbs 10:21 in your Bible or read it here. What does it say about this situation?

> The lips of the righteous nourish many, but fools die for lack of judgment. — Proverbs 10:21

To paraphrase, Proverbs 10:21 says that what righteous people say brings nourishment, but fools die because they lack judgment. When you jump in and hold someone accountable without thought or counsel from the Lord, you can absolutely kill any chances for friendship.

In all four scenarios, the central issue is domination or control. If you are being confronted, you may try to control the situation so that everyone else needs to change instead of you. If you are avoiding confronting someone else, you are also trying to control the situation. You are trying to keep the friendship from ending, so you don't speak truth into someone's life. When you are confronting someone without having permission or without earning the right to speak, then you are also trying to control her. You want that person to do what you think needs to be done. When domination takes over a relationship, there is no positive outcome. In reality, God is the One who needs to control the relationship. He created it, and He knows the plans He has for it. Let go of control and hand it over to the One who can handle it best.

Wrapping It Up

When it comes to making known a possible blind spot in another person, guard the relationship from domination by constantly giving the friendship to God. Place your friendship under His control and let Him lead and guide the relationship. He can do such a better job than we ever could.

Apply It!

Seek Upwardly

Trace your fist in your journal. Then trace your open hand. Over the fist write "control." Over the open hand write "His." Thank God that He is in control of your friendships, not you. If you have been controlling in your friendships, confess that to God and seek His forgiveness. Surrender control back to Him as the only One worthy of that role. Let the course of the friendship be placed in His hands.

Seek Inwardly

On the palm of your hand, write the words "let go." Talk with God about this: Am I controlling? Why? What is going on inside of me that makes me feel that I need to take control? Throughout the day, let this remind you to let go of control in relationships and let God lead instead. If the Spirit of God convicts you to ask forgiveness for trying to control a certain friendship, go and make it right with that friend.

Seek Outwardly

Ask God to help you not annihilate a relationship when it forces you to look at a blind spot. Ask Him to help you not become arrogant, avoid confrontation, or assume a role of accountability that you have not earned. Ask God to help you receive the revealing of a blind spot in your life by a friend, knowing that it will enable you to become more and more like Jesus as you get rid of the compromising area in your life.

Day 3: Heart Check: Pure in Heart

Pray, *Holy Spirit, be my Teacher. Give me understanding on how to put what I learn today into practice. In the name of Jesus I ask, amen.*

. . . .

When it comes to accountability, not only are kind words needed, but pure motives are needed too. If you are not careful, your heart may be misunderstood when you lovingly show another person a blind spot. The focus must not be placed on the blind spot but rather on the growth that can come as Christ molds Himself into that area. The key is in the way you approach your friend with her blind spot.

Open your Bible and read Matthew 5:8. How does this verse relate to friendship and confronting another's blind spot?

> Blessed are the pure in heart, for they will see God. — Matthew 5:8

Go to www.blueletterbible.com and find out what each word means. Record in your journal what you find.

Jesus explained that we will be happy and fortunate when our thoughts, feelings, and desires for our friends are clean (pure). The result of having clear and clean motives is an ability to see a deeper side of God that many never see, because you begin to see others the way He sees them. When our hearts' desires for the ones we love align with the desires of God for their lives, then we see them like God sees them. This clearer vision opens up a depth in our relationship with God that allows us to see Him more clearly for who He is. The more purely we approach others, the more purely we will see God's perfectly pure heart for us. If we were to write this beatitude in our own words, we might write, "Eternally happy are those who willingly offer the condition of their heart before the Lord to cleanse every thought, feeling, and motive, for they will see God in ways they have never imagined."

King Solomon had these words of wisdom to share about purity of heart. Read Proverbs 22:11 in your Bible or here in the book.

> He who loves a pure heart and whose speech is gracious will have the king for his friend. — Proverbs 22:11

King Solomon was saying that anybody who has another's best interests at heart and who speaks blessings to others is a friend of his (a king). If you want to have good, solid friendships, make sure that your heart is pure and that others know your heart toward them is pure.

When your desire is to help your friend see and work through a blind spot, you can communicate that your heart is pure in these ways:

1. *Investing.* In order to hold someone accountable, you must have previously made enough investments in her life to have the right to take some withdrawals. If I go to my bank, I cannot take a withdrawal if I haven't made any deposits. So it is with friendship. You cannot jump in and hold anybody accountable unless you have first made some investments into the friendship, investments that show evidence of genuine love, care, concern, and a willingness to partner with her as long as it takes. If you have deposited no investment and then try to waltz in, hold someone accountable, and then leave, you have dropped a bomb on her and have left her to deal with the casualties. That is not fair and it is not God's plan.

2. *Investigating.* Always approach others with humility and love in an effort to understand their situation. Before rushing to confront them, ask them to help you understand why they have acted in a certain way. This may answer your questions and bring accountability without your ever saying another word.

Read Proverbs 13:15 in your Bible or read it here and then write down in your journal how it relates to confronting a friend.

> Good understanding wins favor, but the way of the unfaithful is hard. —Proverbs 13:15

Your effort to understand others' blind spots expresses that you genuinely care about them and love them. Couple that humility with the acknowledgement that you don't have it all together and don't have all the answers. This will help you partner and will promote growth in both of you.

3. *Inquiring.* Most people do not like accountability unless either they have asked for it or you have graciously offered it. Even if you think you are close enough friends to offer it, giving uninvited accountability might deal a blow to the relationship from which it may never recover. If you feel a friend needs accountability in an area, ask if she would like for you to hold her accountable. If she is not ready, don't push. Pray instead. Proverbs 15:23 says, "How good is a timely word!" Ask God if you should confront, to show you the opportune time to confront, and to make your friend ready for your time together.

Wrapping It Up

Making plenty of investments, investigating the reasons behind behavior, and inquiring of God to direct you every step of the way are critical in shifting the focus from the blind spot to the pure desire of your heart to grow with your friend to be more like Christ. That way, both of your eyes are set on the beneficial results of individual, spiritual, and relational growth for your future.

Apply It!

Seek Upwardly

Record this beatitude (Matthew 5:8) in your journal. Thank God for the confidence in knowing that He is always pure in His dealings with you. Ask God to cleanse and purify your heart—your thoughts, your feelings, and your motives—so you can see Him more fully.

Seek Inwardly

Draw a picture of what you think of when you hear the word *pure*. Talk with God about your heart: Are my motives pure? What motives in my heart are not pure? Ask God to make your heart pure in every way toward Him and toward others. Ask Him to help you consider others before yourself.

Seek Outwardly

Ask God to show you ways to invest in your close friendships so that when withdrawals are necessary, you have earned the right to confront them. Ask Him to show you how to ask the right questions and to give you direction about when (or not) to talk with a friend.

Day 4: No Room for Enmeshment

Pray, *Holy Spirit, be my Teacher. Give me understanding on how to put what I learn today into practice. In the name of Jesus I ask, amen.*

• • • • • • • • •

Okay, I have to be honest and tell you that I struggle with having very high expectations, especially of myself! For example, if I have driven somewhere before and it took me thirty minutes, I compete with myself to get there the next time in twenty-five! Anybody else do that? If you have unrealistic and unhealthy expectations, you will find yourself in constant disappointment with yourself and others.

So often when people seek to control a relationship, their domination can cause others to question themselves. If not careful, they will lose their own distinctiveness because they are working so hard to be what the controlling person is demanding from them. On the other hand, if that same person tries to resist change based on her friend's demands, she will fight so hard to be who she wants to be that she may miss the changes that really do need to take place in her life. Both of these extremes can greatly hinder spiritual growth because both can lead to enmeshment.

Enmeshment occurs when a person gets caught up or entangled in another person's ideal or in their own ideal to the point that both lose their own unique selves. When this happens, the relationship, once established by God for the purpose of growth toward wholeness, will work against the very purpose for which it began.

In many relationships, enmeshment occurs when one person tries to make the other person become like her. She believes her way is right and, thus, whatever is different in a friend's life must be altered to fit her expectations. Enmeshed people fear conflict and try to control others. They usually use anger as their method of control. It looks like this: When they are not in control, they get angry! They give the cold shoulder and withhold love, or they yell and scream and use fear tactics to take back control of their friends. Most don't even realize they are doing it because they have become so accustomed to operating in relationships in this way. It is definitely a blind spot.

Enmeshed relationships also work against God's plan for wholeness when the person being controlled digs in her heels against the one trying to control. When she has had enough of her controlling friend using anger as a means to make her do what she wants, she will fight hard to maintain autonomy. But in this fight, she will miss true blind spots that need to be changed. She will become too consumed with not letting her friend change her. This becomes a blind spot in itself.

The best way to guard against enmeshment is to appreciate one another's differences, to call out one another's blind spots as God leads, and to ditch one's own expectations of how another's responses ought to look. Expectations can be damaging to a relationship. When I say the word *expectation*, I am not talking about obedience to Scripture. When it comes to our friends, our spouses, or others in relationship with us, we definitely ought to be able to expect them to behave in obedience to Scripture. Where things go awry is when we expect others to love, give, and communicate the way we do. We are different people with different personalities and different backgrounds that shape us. For instance, my husband sees love as physical affection. I see love as encouragement. I see faithfulness as keeping my promises. My husband sees it as not having an affair. I may reciprocate friendship by conversation. Others may reciprocate friendship by giving gifts, spending time, or serving. None of these expressions of love is wrong; they are simply different responses made by different people. When you expect all of your friends to respond the way you would and then try to force them to comply, they will begin to resist you because you are trying to make them act like you. And they are not you.

Open your Bible and read Romans 8:29. Then write down in your journal how this verse relates to expectations.

God knew what he was doing from the very beginning. He decided from the outset to shape the lives of those who love him along the same lines as the life of his Son. — Romans 8:29, MSG

God predetermined to conform us to Christ's likeness, not another person's likeness. Put aside your expectations in this regard and let your friends respond to their blind spots in the way God leads them, based on how God has wired them. Appreciate the differences and learn from them.

Wrapping It Up

If God wants to make you like Jesus, then you can encourage and expect others to walk in obedience to the will and ways of Jesus. You cannot, however, expect everyone to respond the same way you would. Don't try to force your friends to be like you. Encourage them to be like Jesus and leave the way that looks to God.

Apply It!

Seek Upwardly

Write Romans 8:29 in your journal. Ask God to help you be conformed to His likeness in every way. Ask Him to show you ways that you might have unrealistic expectations of others. Ask Him to purify your friendships so each person is free to be who He made them to be.

Seek Inwardly

Grab two paper clips of the same size. Attach them so they are connected but you can still see two different clips present. Trace them on your paper and write, "On the same journey as different people." Ask God to help you view your friendships in this way. This puts the blinders on, encouraging us to focus on what God is doing instead of on the blind spots that tend to discourage us.

Seek Outwardly

Thank God for your friends whom you are connected to but whom you are not exactly like. Ask Him to help you appreciate the differences.

You may even want to give the paper clips to a friend or take a picture of the clips and send it to her with a note that tells the differences about her that you appreciate.

Day 5: A Promise to Be Made

Pray, *Holy Spirit, be my Teacher. Give me understanding on how to put what I learn today into practice. In the name of Jesus I ask, amen.*

. . . .

Try to locate a piece of sandpaper and then meditate for a moment on the purpose of it. Sandpaper smoothes out rough edges. Sometimes I call my husband my "heavenly sandpaper" because he grates on my ever-loving nerves! When those moments of sandpapering occur, I have to remind myself that God is using them to make me more like Jesus.

Throughout these two weeks of discussing blind spots and blinders, it has been my prayer that you have seen that God wants you to be whole. He is so committed to your wholeness that He will use His Word and close friends to reveal blind spots so you can deal with them and grow into His likeness. My prayer is that you have seen that He lovingly holds you ACCOUNTABLE and places others in your life to do the same. He offers COURAGEOUS ENCOURAGEMENT to help you face difficult places in your life so that holiness can be forged within you. I pray you have determined to respond to His revealing of truth as He holds you accountable to His Word. I hope you will listen when your closest friends reveal a blind spot. I hope you will reciprocate out of a pure heart, giving your friends strength to face their blind spots. And I pray you will free others to let God use them to encourage change in your behavior while holding on to your individuality. This will build closeness between you and God and between you and your close friends. This will make facing blind spots easier to handle because you share the load with a friend.

This week we have spent a lot of time on what we do not need to give others, namely a controlling attitude and enmeshment. What we do need to give others is freedom. Open your Bible and read Galatians 5:1. Rewrite this verse in your own words in your journal.

It is for freedom that Christ has set us free. Stand firm, then, and do not let yourselves be burdened again by a yoke of slavery. — Galatians 5:1

A focus on our blind spots can cause us to become enslaved to our inadequacies; that can become an extremely heavy load to bear. The antidote is to ask God and others to help us remove the blind spots in our lives so we can live in the freedom that He promised us. To keep from being weighed down by what you are not, keep the focus on what you are becoming and the freedom that comes with it. Put on your blinders and place them on your friends as well. Together, focus on the freedom that believers can enjoy. Give your friends the freedom to be truly free.

May I suggest we all make this commitment as we seek to remove blind spots and place Blinders on our friendships?

"I will partner in my friends' spiritual growth."

This means you will commit to helping a friend work through her blind spots and focus on the freedom that God promises to bring. In a world where many people carry a heavy load of guilt and condemnation, one of the greatest gifts you can give is the freedom to be what God made her to be as she surrenders herself to His lordship. Lift the load!

With that commitment comes the responsibility to lovingly approach her with her blind spots in a way that promotes growth, not resentment, anger, or insecurity. You will do this when you invest, investigate, and inquire of God and of your friend about how you can help her. When your friend and God answer, be faithful to respond. That will show your commitment to her wholeness.

The beauty in this commitment is that God has made the same commitment to you: **"I will partner in your spiritual growth."**

Read John 14:16 in your Bible or in this book. In your journal, record what this verse says about God's commitment to your spiritual growth.

> I will ask the Father, and he will give you another Counselor to be with you forever. — John 14:16

The word *counselor* is the Greek word *parakletos*, and it means "one called alongside to help." God has not left us alone to fix the blind spots in our lives. He gave His Spirit to come alongside and help us.

Wrapping It Up

God truly is our "heavenly sandpaper," but He gives us dear friends who can also help us sand down our rough edges that don't resemble Jesus. When you choose to offer partnership to your friends, you are showing them "Jesus with skin on." How awesome to think that God would grant us that privilege and responsibility as a friend. As you take on this role, you truly are becoming a disciple of Jesus Christ as you do exactly what He does.

As this week draws to a close, ask the Holy Spirit to help you put into practice what you learned; ask in the name of Jesus.

Apply It!

Seek Upwardly

Write this friendship commitment in your journal and refer to it today and in the days to come. Write out John 14:16 and thank God for the Spirit who helps you.

Ask God to help you partner in others' spiritual growth.

Seek Inwardly

Take some time to write in your journal about what stuck out to you as God revealed Himself to you this week. Write down how this truth has affected your relational views of God and others, as well as how it will change the way you live in relationship with God and others.

Seek Outwardly
Begin to approach friends with a pure heart, reasonable expectations, and partnership when dealing with their blind spots. Put aside control, anger, and enmeshment, and help others focus on the freedom that comes from being who God created them to be.

Ask God to help you come alongside your friends and help them focus on all that God is doing in their lives. Help them see how far they've come so they can rejoice and be motivated to continue.

week 7

the possibilities (part 1)

Day 1: Affection

Pray, *Holy Spirit, be my Teacher. Give me understanding on how to put what I learn today into practice. In the name of Jesus I ask, amen.*

. . . .

Numerous Scriptures tell us that when it comes to visioning with God, the possibilities are endless! Jesus Himself said, "What is impossible with men is possible with God" (Luke 18:27).

As we come to our last two weeks, we enter the final level in friendship called **The Possibilities.** How blessed we become when God has brought into our lives intimate friends who genuinely care about us and want us to become all that God created us to be. These friends truly see our potential and want to help explore all the possible ways God might use us. These friendships are rare and should be treasured.

One of the ways that you demonstrate your friendship at this intimate level of relationship is by being **AFFECTIONATE,** showing a deep fondness for another person. God has given you a love for others—even in their faults and flaws—that can be explained only by Him. This is a **COHESIVE LOVE**—a deep, mutually reciprocated love that acts like a glue to hold the friendship together even through the roughest of times. Throughout the study, we have talked about puzzle pieces and how they are connected. Most puzzle pieces have four sides with which to connect. If the four sides to your life's "puzzle piece" represent your friends, "your four" are those who are a part of this deepest level of friendship.

This depth of friendship parallels with God's affection for you. God doesn't just love you; He likes you! He likes you a lot! He is even more committed to seeing you fulfill the purposes for which He created you than you are. He knows His exact purpose for creating you, and He will stop at nothing to help you find it. He loves you so much that He will stick it out with you no matter what comes your way, because He sees the potential in you that maybe you don't even see yourself. That's where intimate friends come in. God graces you with them to help you see the possibilities in yourself that you can't see. And God desires for you to deeply love others enough to stick it out through the good times and bad to help them reach their full potential.

Because many people have never experienced this kind of love, it seems foreign. Some people feel like such deep love can be achieved only through some kind of sexual expression. Deep affection for others has been so twisted by the world that we cannot comprehend an intimate love without some physical expression. Because we have such an insatiable desire for the feeling of being deeply loved, many people who do not have the correct understanding of relationships will try to find that deep love in any way possible. Music, television, books, magazines, and movies portray that deep affection can be experienced only through sexual encounters. The world acts like an animal in heat — sex-focused, sex-consumed, and sex-crazed.

Yet Scripture provides a very different picture of healthy platonic affection. In 2 Samuel 1, David grieved over the death of his beloved friend, Jonathan. In verse 26, David said, "I grieve for you, Jonathan my brother; you were very dear to me. Your love for me was wonderful, more wonderful than that of women." Some people claim that this verse is proof that David and Jonathan were in a homosexual relationship. Is this true? Was David gay? Absolutely not! David had several wives whom he loved very much. Besides, if the two were in a sexual relationship, David wouldn't have called Jonathan a brother; he would have called him a lover. So why would David say that Jonathan's love toward him was better than that of women? Because David was referring to love as more than a physical act. The sexual act of loving a woman was temporary. The supportive act of genuinely loving a brother was eternal. Sexual expression is a small part of the big picture of love, and yet most people have boiled love down to sex alone, missing the fullness that sincere love offers.

When God gives a man a deep love for a woman, that man is to make a covenant of loyalty to her, and God allows the couple the privilege of the sexual act to signify their never-ending covenant. This physical act is a symbol of the spiritual truth that Jesus is the Bridegroom and believers are His bride.

He showed His never-ending commitment to us by paying the price for our sin, which was death. Taking our punishment, He offered His hand in "marriage" — union and communion — to you. Upon acceptance, you took on His name, "Christian," and He responded by offering you eternal life, a new heart, and all the treasures of heaven as expressions of His never-ending covenant. And just as a husband "enters into" his wife sexually, Jesus enters into us through His Holy Spirit — a gift and sign solely for His bride — as evidence of His unfailing love and commitment. Others outside of the marriage can be intimate friends with whom you can be appropriately affectionate, but no one else gets this private, personal, and highly sacred and symbolic gift of sex. Physical union is to be regarded as sacred, reserved for only one man with one woman, just as Jesus asks for your hand in marriage personally, just between you and Him.

The apostle Peter also addressed deep love between friends (without sex) in 1 Peter 1:22. Open your Bible and read this verse. Consider what loving another deeply looks like.

Now that you have purified yourselves by obeying the truth so that you have sincere love for your brothers, love one another deeply, from the heart. — 1 Peter 1:22

Peter later supported this idea throughout his letter (see 2:17; 3:8; 4:8). What does that kind of love look like? Many of us have never seen it or experienced it. It is the love of Jesus flowing back and forth through two friends. It is a love that originates and culminates in Jesus. It is a 1 Corinthians 13 kind of love (love is patient, love is kind, and so forth) that you can offer only as Jesus loves *through* you.

My family had the privilege of going on a mission trip to Ethiopia. While there, we saw Christlike love demonstrated within every relationship among the people. We witnessed deep affection, or liking and caring, among all of them. They were patient, helpful, caring, supportive, kind, courteous, encouraging, forgiving, humble, and teachable. As a result, these men and women showed appropriate affection to each other. Men stood around arm in arm, hugging as they greeted each other with smiles that stretched across their faces. If we saw men doing that in America, we would quickly jump to the conclusion that they must be gay. Those of us in the United States may develop fondness or affection for others, but because we have not embraced or exemplified Christlike love, we don't respond with appropriate affection. Fear of being falsely accused keeps us from being affectionate. As a result, we further isolate ourselves and are starved from the benefits that human touch brings. That fear coupled with the twisted mind-set that love equals sex has caused our nation to become sexually obsessed, yet still unhappy and dissatisfied. A world without Christlike love is missing the full experience of love, trading it in for a facade that will never fully satisfy.

Wrapping It Up

God wants us to know His deep affection for us. He truly loves us and is committed to our best interests. His love is a cohesive love that sticks with us no matter what. He wants us to exemplify that love to those around us, building strong bonds that speak life, courage, and confidence.

Apply It!

Seek Upwardly

Look up Proverbs 18:24 and write it in your journal. Thank God for His cohesive love that sticks closer than any brother ever could. Draw a picture in your journal of a peanut butter and jelly sandwich or anything else that might represent something sticky. Express your desire to stick closely to God and ask Him to help you do that.

Seek Inwardly

Ask God to make you a friend who sticks close to your intimate friends. Write 1 Peter 1:22 in your journal. Think about your friendships: Do I love with my limited love or with God's love? How can I learn to love like Jesus loves? Surrender your life to allow the Lord to love your friends through you and to train you in His love.

Seek Outwardly

If you are in a group, you might want to take a picture of something that is sticky and text it to the other members. It will be a sweet reminder of sticking closely to your friends and to God. You might even want to forward the text to an intimate friend and tell her that you love her and will stick with her no matter what, helping her fulfill the purposes for which God made her.

Day 2: Beware the Dangers of Disapproval

Pray, *Holy Spirit, be my Teacher. Give me understanding on how to put what I learn today into practice. In the name of Jesus I ask, amen.*

· · · · · · · · ·

By the time most friendships reach this level of intimacy, both know each other very well, and both desperately want the other to work through her past and her blind spots so that she can move forward with God and do what He created her to do. However, if these friends are not careful, they will become impatient with a friend who is not maturing and growing as quickly as they wanted. They may show this frustration in a variety of ways, but the result is the same: a feeling of condemnation. When a friend is condemning, she makes you feel as though she is totally disappointed with you and totally disapproves of you. This can lead to performance-based living and an unhealthy focus on pleasing another person rather than pleasing God. That is idolatry, and God says He will not have it.

In friendship, the negative qualities you see in another person are simply their positive qualities being twisted and misused. For example, you may have a friend who is extremely critical of others. In that instance, the God-given gift of discernment is being misused. God has given her the ability to see the flaws and blind spots in others so she can know how to pray for them, encourage them, and help them. But this gift can be twisted and used to condemn them by being critical of them and even talking about them. See how it works?

Here are some other examples: Someone who is extremely controlling, arrogant, and overbearing actually has the God-given gifts of leadership and confidence that are being misused. A friend who is extremely passive and indecisive may have the God-given gift of flexibility and cooperativeness. The friend who procrastinates has a God-given gift of patience and a submissive spirit. And finally, the friend who is impatient, pushy, stubborn, and perfectionistic is really one who has the God-given gifts of zeal, discipline, persuasiveness, and efficiency.

So what is the solution? How do we help them get these negative characteristics untwisted?

1. Bring attention to the positive more often than the negative. When a friend uses the characteristic positively, commend her for it. Say things such as, "The way you have the ability to _____ (positive character trait) is amazing. I see God at work in you when you live like that. You would make such a great _____ (fill in with an occupation, ministry, service, or so on)!" In this way, you are turning her attention to the positive qualities. That shifting of focus changes the approach and the attitude, which then begins to transform the actions.

2. Think of and design activities that develop that characteristic in a positive manner within your friend. Watch for opportunities for her to use these positive qualities and encourage her to step in and use them in the right way. Look for an opening in the community for her to volunteer. Offer to do it with her. Who knows, God may use you to transform her direction in life to conform to God's original design for her!

Open your Bible and read Hebrews 10:24. Summarize it in light of what you've learned today.

> And let us consider how we may spur one another on toward love and good deeds. — Hebrews 10:24

The word *spur* means "to arouse, incite, and provoke in order to sharpen." Part of your role as an intimate friend is to incite your friend to use her God-given qualities the way God intended.

Wrapping It Up

When helping your friend discover the possibilities that await her, you may be tempted to become disappointed when you see her negative character traits. To protect yourself from condemning your friend, help her untwist the negative uses of her God-given qualities and sharpen them into a tool God can use to cut through the darkness and help others see the light and life of Jesus shining through.

Apply It!

Seek Upwardly

Look up Proverbs 27:17 and write it in your journal. Thank God for giving you a character that reflects Him. Ask Him to help you use it to give others an accurate representation of Him. Thank the Lord for friends who will come alongside you and help sharpen your Christlike character qualities.

Seek Inwardly

Grab a knife from your kitchen. Place it where you'll see it throughout the day to remind you about the sharpening of your intimate friends. Ask the Lord to reveal misused character in your intimate friends and to give you wisdom about how to help them use it in the way He intended.

Seek Outwardly

Ask God to make you open to receiving help from your intimate friends as they see all the incredible possibilities that lay ahead of you. Surrender yourself to God's loving hand to sharpen you through an intimate friend, as iron sharpens iron. Think of a way you can spur your friends on, and then do that for them today. For with God, nothing is impossible!

Day 3: Heart Check: Peacemaker

Pray, *Holy Spirit, be my Teacher. Give me understanding on how to put what I learn today into practice. In the name of Jesus I ask, amen.*

• • • • • • • • •

Conflict is not an *if* but a *when*. Would you agree?

Conflict is inevitable in relationships. Conflict is a given. Wherever two people are, there are two different perspectives, biases, upbringings, bents, and pasts. At some point, one or all of these are going to collide. The result is conflict.

Conflict grows and changes with age. As children, we have conflicts over not sharing our things or breaking someone else's toy. As adults, we experience conflict over deeper issues, such as not fully sharing our hearts or breaking one another's trust. When we take off our masks and give others the freedom to call out our blind spots and help us untwist our misused character qualities, there is bound to be some disagreements and misunderstandings.

Jesus knew all too well that this would happen. Open your Bible and read Matthew 5:9. Meditate about how what Jesus said applies to friendship.

> Blessed are the peacemakers, for they will be called sons of God.
> —Matthew 5:9

Go to www.blueletterbible.com to find out what each word means.

Jesus was telling His disciples to get along with others. He knew that with the different personalities among the motley crew, conflict was inevitable; they would need to work through all of their differences and remain a unified group if they were going to take the gospel to the entire world.

A peacemaker is one who works to make peace. She seeks to

cooperate with others and show others how to do the same. The reward promised for the peacemakers is to be called sons of God!

When I read that promise, I was reminded about how many times parents are told that their children look, speak, or act just like them. It's sweet and endearing but also convicting. Sometimes children say and do things like their parents, but their parents wish they didn't. People know that their children are theirs because they look, speak, or act like them. Jesus said that when you seek to be a peacemaker, there is no denying that you are His child.

Ephesians 2:14-18 says,

> For he [Christ] himself is our peace, who has made the two one and has destroyed the barrier, the dividing wall of hostility, by abolishing in his flesh the law with its commandments and regulations. His purpose was to create in himself one new man out of the two, thus making peace, and in this one body to reconcile both of them to God through the cross, by which he put to death their hostility. He came and preached peace to you who were far away and peace to those who were near. For through him we both have access to the Father by one Spirit. — Ephesians 2:14-18

What do you think that means for your relationships?

Jesus came to be our peace. He made peace with God when God's wrath was upon us as sinners. Jesus came to bring peace between the Jew and the Gentile, the slave and the free, and the man and the woman so we could all live in unity with no favoritism or partiality. That's the peace Jesus came to create. When you seek this kind of peace and encourage others to live in that peace, you look just like Jesus.

The most important thing to remember as a peacemaker is that every conflict is an opportunity for Christ to be formed to a greater degree in both people. God never wants conflict to go to waste. He has a purpose for it: to grow people into more of His image. When you face a conflict, keep before you the question, "Lord, what do You want to teach me through this?" This teachable attitude is essential for spiritual growth in your relationships.

Also remember that there are two sides to every coin and both have equal value. Both sides of a conflict have value; both stories need to be heard, and both people must seek to understand the other's perspective.

As you keep these two things in mind, you may be convicted of a sin in a relationship that you need to make right. If so, own it. Don't avoid it or try to throw it off on the other person. Own the part you played in the breakdown of the friendship and make it right by doing these things:

1. Confessing your sin to the one you hurt
2. Apologizing and asking for her forgiveness
3. Accepting and working through the consequences that your sin has caused in the relationship
4. Making restitution where you can
5. Patiently moving through the process of reconciliation

When you do this and help others learn how to do the same, you are a peacemaker. You will be blessed to be called a true daughter of God as people say, "She looks and acts just like her Daddy!"

Wrapping It Up

Romans 12:18 says, "If it is possible, as far as it depends on you, live at peace with everyone." If you want intimate friendships that endure the tests of time, learn how to be a peacemaker. You will need to use that skill at some point in every relationship. Be obedient to do your part and let God handle the rest.

Apply It!

Seek Upwardly

Draw a peace sign in your journal and write out this beatitude beside your drawing. Thank Jesus for coming and making peace with God on your behalf so you could be in relationship with Him. Thank Him that you don't have to fight to prove that you are as good as everyone else because He already did that when He died for you.

Seek Upwardly

Think of a current conflict you are experiencing. Ask God to help you own your sin and do what His Word tells you to do to make it right. Consider with Him what He desires to change in you through this conflict. Humble yourself and let Him do His work in your life.

Seek Outwardly

Ask the Lord to help you become a peacemaker with your friends. Ask Him to help you cooperate with others and use you to teach others how to cooperate. Don't wait for a friend to start the reconciliation process. Be the first to make peace and trust God to help you in the process.

Day 4: No Room for Withholding Honesty

Pray, *Holy Spirit, be my Teacher. Give me understanding on how to put what I learn today into practice. In the name of Jesus I ask, amen.*

. . . .

When my daughter was little, she "helped" me carry in my groceries, dragging a two-liter Dr Pepper up every bump of my stairs. She then proceeded to open the Dr Pepper. Need I tell you what happened? Yep. Too much pressure and it spews everywhere!

One of the biggest mistakes that can be made as a friendship becomes more intimate is to withhold from your friend how you are feeling. When your friend is helping you work through difficulties you have uncovered, blind spots that have surfaced, and character traits that are being misused, tension can begin to creep in. Both of you may feel it, but you may be too afraid to address it for fear of a big blowup. To keep the tension level down and the relationship intact, you may be tempted to hide how you feel. You may even say you're fine when that is really not the case. When dishonesty creeps in, look out. There's a storm brewing ahead. The very thing you were trying to avoid, you may have made worse!

Have you ever found yourself caught in a relationship involving three people? The old saying, "Two's company; three's a crowd" can certainly ring true when you're caught in the middle. Here's an example of what may occur:

You and a friend have become very close. Your roommate does not like your best friend and constantly talks badly about her. Your best friend knows your roommate does not like her and does not know what to do. This conflict becomes an obsession to your best friend because she so wants to be liked. You don't want to lose either friendship and feel caught in the middle. So in an effort to keep both friendships, you don't tell either that you feel torn. At some point, your friend and roommate may force you to pick a side. If that happens, more than likely you will lose one (or both!) of the friendships.

This is just an example of what happens when we are not completely honest with our feelings. Not being totally open about what's going on inside causes chaos and confusion in relationships. When you withhold the truth and don't share your feelings, you leave your friend with the task of figuring it out on her own, and usually her conclusion and response is less helpful than if you had been honest. If you're not careful, the dishonesty will cause expectations and assumptions to creep in. Left unchecked, the relationship will spiral downward until one of you bails on the friendship.

Have you ever experienced something like this? Ever experienced the ramifications of someone who has experienced this? It's not good. The fizz just keeps bubbling up.

Open your Bible and read Proverbs 11:1. Journal what you think this has to do with being honest.

> The LORD abhors dishonest scales, but accurate weights are his delight. — Proverbs 11:1

In biblical times, merchants sold grain or metals by using weights and scales. A buyer would place the merchandise on one side of the scale and their money on the other side until the scale balanced. When the scale balanced, that was the amount required as payment. Dishonest merchants would secretly add weight to the merchandise side of the scale, causing the buyer to get less and pay more. However, once buyers discovered the dishonesty, the merchant lost everything and was alienated from the rest of the people.

God says He hates dishonesty, but honesty brings Him great joy. God delights in your being honest about your feelings no matter what repercussions may result. It's in your best interests too. Relationships can't grow without honesty. It builds a deep sense of trust and growth. Dishonesty breeds mistrust, which destroys the relationship.

Wrapping It Up

If you want intimate friendships that help you reach your God-given potential, you must resist the temptation to withhold your true feelings out of fear. The friendship started off with full disclosure as you took down your cover-ups. Don't cover up your feelings when it feels more vulnerable, risky, or intense. Live a life of integrity. Be honest. Others will be drawn to that kind of relationship.

Apply It!

Seek Upwardly

Draw a set of scales in your journal and write Proverbs 11:1 beside it. Tell God throughout the day that you want to be an honest person who brings Him delight.

Seek Inwardly

Talk with God about a certain circumstance you are currently experiencing that requires honesty: How do I speak honestly and still not hurt feelings? Where have I not been completely honest? What is holding me back? Why? Ask God to help you communicate honestly how you feel about people, beliefs, convictions, and your friendships. Ask God to give you the grace to press through your fears and share openly with love. Then entrust your friendships into God's hands.

Seek Outwardly

Have a conversation with your intimate friends, expressing your desire for them to be honest with you. Communicate that their honesty will not cause you to walk away from the friendship even when it gets hard. Explain that you want to grow into Christlikeness and need to hear the hard things even if they hurt. You may even want to have this conversation over a good cold glass of Dr Pepper!

Day 5: A Promise to Be Made

Pray, *Holy Spirit, be my Teacher. Give me understanding on how to put what I learn today into practice. In the name of Jesus I ask, amen.*

. . . .

It has been my prayer throughout this week on Possibilities that you have seen that God is faithfully committed to your fulfilling the purposes for which He created you. He will use your intimate friends to help steer you in the right direction. My prayer is that you have seen that He is deeply AFFECTIONATE toward you and offers you His COHESIVE LOVE as the One who will always stick close beside you. I hope you can see how God gifts you with intimate friends who can help you see and experience all that He intends for you. I pray that you can protect your friendships from frustration and condemnation by seeing others' negative qualities as positive ones being misused. I hope that you will encourage your friends to turn those into positive traits as you speak into their lives and even design activities that promote the positive traits in them. I also pray that you are open to letting them do the same for you. I pray that you have decided to be a peacemaker, doing whatever you can do to keep peace when conflicts arise and tempt you to walk away. And I pray that as a peacemaker, you will commit to be honest with your feelings so you and your friends can deal with the truth.

This week you have jumped into the weighty issues that you may face as friendships become more intimate. Friendships can flow like the ocean waves, pressing in one day and backing off another. Through it all, the goal is helping your friends reach their full, God-designed potential. Above all that has been discussed this week, there is no greater need than for you to keep others grounded in who they are and who God intended them to be.

Let's catch up on the story of David and Saul. By the time we reach 1 Samuel 23, David has already been anointed king instead of Saul. In this chapter, we find David hiding out from Saul, who was trying to kill him out of a jealous rage. As you remember, King Saul's son Jonathan and David were best friends. In verse 14, the Bible says that David was hiding out in the desert hills and King Saul could not find him. But guess what? Verse 16 says that Jonathan went to David. That is a beautiful thing. Don't miss it. God knows what we need when we need it, and though King Saul and his best men couldn't find David, God knew David needed his friend and allowed Jonathan to find him. God will do the same for you.

Then the Bible says that Jonathan helped David "find strength in God" (verse 16). That phrase implies that Jonathan was reconnecting David's hand to God's. It was as if David had let go of it somewhere along the way and Jonathan came to help David find it again. Jonathan reminded David that Saul would not succeed in killing him because God had anointed him as king. David had forgotten God's plan for his life, but Jonathan had to come remind him.

This is ultimately what a best friend does. She makes sure that others never lose sight of the plan God has for their lives and helps them stay connected to God when the enemies of life send them running for cover.

May I suggest we all make this commitment as we seek to discover and then live out The Possibilities God has for us and our friends?

"I will provide reminders of who my friends are."

This means that you will help your friends discover who they were created to be and provide emotional support as they journey to get there. Come what may, you will stick with them, clasping their hands to God's and reminding them of who they are whenever necessary. In a world where selfishness dominates our society, the selflessness displayed through this gesture is a priceless treasure.

As you commit to join with friends to help them fulfill God's purposes, you also commit to lovingly help them redirect misused God-given qualities. Though conflict may arise, you will seek to keep peace and be honest with your feelings so that true growth can occur and your friends can reach their full potential.

The beauty in this commitment is that God has made this same commitment to you: **"I will provide reminders of who you are."**

Open your Bible and read Ephesians 2:10. Meditate on its truth about how God created you. Record your thoughts in your journal.

> For we are God's workmanship, created in Christ Jesus to do good works, which God prepared in advance for us to do. —Ephesians 2:10

Notice that it says God prepared good works for you to do before you were even born. God did not create you and then sit around with the Trinity and Gabriel to decide what He would make of you. "Let's see . . . what can I do with *her*?" No, God knew what kind of person He would need to help fulfill part of His plan. He planned the work to be done and then He made you to fit the work hand in glove. That knowledge makes me want to find my purpose and do it with all my heart! How about you?

While writing this week, I had the privilege of watching the movie *Hugo*. In the movie, Hugo makes this statement: "I'd imagine the whole world was one big machine. Machines never come with any extra parts, you know. They always come with the exact amount they need. So I figured, if the entire world was one big machine, I couldn't be an extra part. I had to be here for some reason."[1]

Every person God created has great purpose. When you choose to partner with God in helping a friend reach her full potential, you are showing her Jesus' heart. How awesome to think that God would grant us that privilege and responsibility as a friend. As you take on this role, you truly are becoming Christ's disciple, as you do exactly what He does.

---

1. John Logan, *Hugo*, directed by Martin Scorsese (Hollywood, CA: Paramount Pictures, 2011).

Wrapping It Up

As you close out your week, ask the Holy Spirit to be your Teacher and to give you understanding and wisdom to put into practice what you learned this week; ask in the name of Jesus.

Apply It!

Seek Upwardly

Write this friendship commitment in your journal and refer to it today and in the days to come. Write out Ephesians 2:10 in your journal as well and thank God for making you with a specific plan in mind. Ask Him to help you fulfill it.

Seek Inwardly

Take some time to write in your journal about what stuck out to you as God revealed Himself to you this week. Write down how this truth has affected your relational views of God and others, as well as how it will change the way you live in relationship with God and others.

Seek Outwardly

Begin to see others as people with great purpose. Learn to see negative characteristics as positive ones being twisted and misused. Put aside condemnation when others are maturing more slowly than you would like, and seek peace in the process. Be honest with your feelings and help your friends' hands stay firmly grasped to God's, reminding them of who they are and who God created them to be.

Ask God to help you come alongside your friends and help them focus on all that God is doing in their lives. Help them see how far they've come so they can rejoice and be motivated to continue.

the possibilities (part 2)

Day 1: Action

Pray, *Holy Spirit, be my Teacher. Give me understanding on how to put what I learn today into practice. In the name of Jesus I ask, amen.*

· · · · · · · · ·

You have heard the old adage "actions speak louder than words." So often words are not supported by actions. We say a lot of things, but our lives don't reflect that we truly believe those things we say. This lack of consistency is one of the major indictments against the church, because believers say they believe God's Word but obey only parts of it. This discrepancy leaves people uneasy and skeptical about a genuine relationship with Jesus. The same applies in our friendships. If our words are not supported by our actions, it causes the friendship to be shaky and questionable.

By the time friendships make it to this level, much has been uncovered, revealed, and worked through. Like the transformation of a caterpillar to a butterfly, your friendship with God and others has morphed as well. In the process, your journey toward Christlikeness has come into better view, along with the specific mission God created you to accomplish. As God has revealed through others your great potential, you can choose to begin to try out your new wings. As this happens, all kinds of fearful thoughts can run through your head. At this point, we need our friends to be **ACTIONARY**. We need them in our corner, cheering us on, having our backs. But we also need to be acting on our behalf, as the word implies: *Actionary* means "something *done* as opposed to something *said*."

As you step into your God-given purposes, you need an intimate friend who will offer **COMMITTED CONFIDENCE** in you. That friend will not only speak of her commitment to you, but her actions will also support that verbal affirmation. This tangible support will give you an immeasurable amount of confidence to spread your wings as you head toward fulfilling your destiny.

When God called me to write these discipleship resources, I felt extremely inadequate. I even told God that He picked the wrong person to write them. Yet when God began to prompt friends to speak into my life about the specific Christlike qualities they saw in me and then backed that by helping me design, organize, plan, and implement how these resources would get into the hands of those who needed them, a confidence rose in me.

I am so thankful that God is our example of being actionary. He didn't just tell us He loved us; He showed us He loved us.

Open your Bible and read Romans 5:8. How did God's actions mirror His words?

> But God demonstrates his own love for us in this: While we were still sinners, Christ died for us. — Romans 5:8

God, through Jesus, was committed to love us all the way to the cross and now sits at the right hand of God praying for us, still committed to us. Now if that doesn't give us all some confidence to step into what He's called us to, I don't know what will! God is faithful to finish what He started in you (see Philippians 1:6).

Wrapping It Up

As your intimate friends begin to spread their wings and attempt to live out their God-given destinies, they will need your encouragement, not just in word but also in deeds. Your commitment will blow just enough wind of confidence into their wings to help them go places they've never dared try to venture before.

Apply It!

Seek Upwardly

Thank God for His committed confidence in you. You may want to draw a picture of a cross in your journal. Then record Romans 5:8 in your journal and ask God what He wants to say to you. Listen for a few minutes and then write down what He says. He may say something such as, "I am for you. You can do what I'm asking of you. I am right here with you. I've got this!" Thank Jesus for dying for you because He believed in you and God's purposes for you.

Seek Inwardly

Ask God to show you what action to take to begin fulfilling the purposes for which He made you. Let Him guide you through every step in that journey. Learn to listen for His voice directing you. Tell Him that you don't just want to say you love Him but that you want to prove it through your actions, just like He did.

Seek Outwardly

Ask God to reveal how you can take action to show your intimate friends that you support them and are committed to them becoming all that God intended for them. Then walk in obedience even if it makes no sense to you. God has a plan, and He will ask of you what He needs in order to give your friends the committed confidence they need.

Day 2: Beware the Dangers of Disputes

Pray, *Holy Spirit, be my Teacher. Give me understanding on how to put what I learn today into practice. In the name of Jesus I ask, amen.*

• • • • • • • • •

From sporting events to grades in school, society has set us up for competition. While some competition is healthy, some is destructive.

As you and your intimate friends focus on becoming all that God designed you to become, you can be sure that the temptation to compete and compare will rear its ugly head. While healthy evaluation makes for good accountability, it can slip into an unhealthy silent dispute about who is the best. This has ruined the best of friendships.

Imagine a mother who is very sick. She gathers her two daughters around her to explain that she will soon die a very painful death. Then imagine that almost immediately, her children start asking if they can claim some of the things she will leave behind, like her furniture, her car, her vintage china, and even her home. Picture both daughters as they begin to fight over who deserves what and why. Would you find this rude? Inappropriate? Sad? Immature? Inconsiderate? Disrespectful? Dishonoring?

Something very similar happened to Jesus, and it is recorded in Mark 9. He had predicted His death, and the disciples got into a dispute over who was the greatest. Jesus answered them all by saying, "If anyone wants to be first, he must be the very last, and the servant of all" (verse 35).

Later on, Jesus again shared with His beloved disciples that He would soon die a brutal death, and again, they jumped into the same dispute.

Mark 10:43-45 contains Jesus' response. Look it up in your Bible and think about the implications His response has on your life.

Whoever wants to become great among you must be your servant, and whoever wants to be first must be slave of all. For even the Son of Man did not come to be served, but to serve, and to give his life as a ransom for many. — Mark 10:43-45

Jesus was with these disciples and taught them how to live like Him and for Him, and even *they* had these disputes. Therefore, you can rest assured that this temptation can creep into your thoughts as well. In both accounts, Jesus gave the same answer: The greatest will be the one who serves. Notice that Jesus did not say it was wrong to strive for excellence. Of course He wants you to be your best. He just doesn't want you to try to be someone else's best. God wants you to excel at what He made *you* to do and be. The only one you can compete with is yourself, because there is no one like you. The only measure by which you can realistically compare yourself is God's Word, because everyone is on her own specific journey with the Father. We are all at different places in the journey—not ahead or behind, just different.

Pursuing excellence is not a sin in itself. Paul encouraged us to run our race of life in such a way as to win (see 1 Corinthians 9:24). Striving to be more becomes bad when your misplaced competition and comparisons cause you to sacrifice everyone else on the altar of selfishness and ego along the way. Jesus wants us to understand that instead of needing to be noticed as the greatest, we need to take notice of the needs of those around us. Serving instead of always demanding to be served will bring true greatness in the end.

In this story in Mark 10, Jesus used the word *slave*. It is the Greek word *doulas*, and it means a "bond slave." Understanding that word requires a little Old Testament history lesson. Exodus 21 records that if a man bought a slave and if that slave married and had sons and daughters, after seven years of serving his master, the slave could go free. However, he had to leave his wife and children with that master.

But if the slave wanted to, he could go to court and declare that even though he could rightfully go free, he was choosing to remain a slave and stay with his wife and children. At that point, he took on the marking of his master in the form of an earring, and he remained a slave for the rest of his life, completely yielding his rights to his master.

When Jesus talked about being a slave, He was saying that though we could choose to live freely for ourselves, the greatest will choose to remain under the Master's service, giving to others in total selflessness. In our relationship with God and others, we must choose daily (and sometimes moment by moment) whether to serve or to be served, whether to be a free woman or a slave to Christ's love and obedience.

Wrapping It Up

As you seek to fulfill the purposes for which God made you, and as your intimate friend does the same, guard yourselves against competition and comparison that leads to disputes over who is the best. Shift your focus from competing with each other to serving each other and those around you.

Rejoice at your friend's successes, knowing that she is on her path and you are on yours. Even when you help create opportunities for your friend to use her gifts, don't be jealous when she succeeds; instead, be happy that she is fulfilling God's purposes for her life. This "least" mentality looks like the greatest to your Father.

Apply It!

Seek Upwardly

Draw a set of chains or handcuffs in your journal and write Mark 10:43-45 beside it. Commit to remain a bond slave of Jesus Christ, choosing to serve others around you. Thank Jesus for becoming a bond slave for you, taking the markings of His Master — nail-scarred hands and feet.

Seek Inwardly

Discuss with God if you are an unhealthy competitor: Do I have my eyes on people insead of Him? Why do I always feel the need to be better than everybody else instead of just striving to be my best? Determine to outserve those around you. Make this your new healthy competition. Run this race for the prize of being the greatest by becoming the least.

Seek Outwardly

Ask God to show you places and people to serve. Ask Him to help you be obedient when He reveals them to you. Act on what He tells you to do.

Day 3: Heart Check: Persecuted

Pray, *Holy Spirit, be my Teacher. Give me understanding on how to put what I learn today into practice. In the name of Jesus I ask, amen.*

· · · · · · · · ·

In week 5, we talked about the dangers of discouragement, especially when working through the blind spots in our life. This week, we need to talk about the dangers of discouragers. Discouragers are those people who will not let you spread your wings and fly. They want to keep you caged up. Some even try to clip your wings, so to speak. You can probably picture those people in your mind. We need to see them for who they are and know what God says about them.

If you have ever watched *Wipeout* or *America's Funniest Home Videos*, you know how funny it is to see someone falling out of control. Take a minute to locate some video clips of people falling and have yourself a good belly laugh. (We need those every once in a while.)

It is funny to watch people fall, especially when we know they were not injured in the process. My husband especially loves watching funny videos of those falls. Over the years, I have taken more joy in observing my husband watch them than in watching the videos themselves. My husband gets so tickled when he sees people out of control and falling. Not too long ago he fell himself, and our children and I nearly died laughing! There is actually a term for this: My husband engages in *schadenfreude*, which means taking great delight in the misfortune of others.

While falls can be harmless, we can land on a slippery slope and crash if we are not careful. Many people head down a very slippery slope that begins with their own lack of success. Because they didn't "make it," or achieve their potential, they don't want anyone else to succeed either. So they seek to ruin others' chances of success. They even take great delight in seeing others fail. They engage in *schadenfreude*. That slippery slope can move from *schadenfreude* to narcissism if their selfish egos go unchecked.

People may be obtaining *schadenfreude* from one of your friends. To combat those people, you may want to suggest that your friend consider removing or at least distancing herself from those who are not promoting her success. You can also be her biggest fan as she overcomes the negative influence of those people.

When people seek to discourage us from God's calling on our lives, they could travel down the slippery slope from discouraging us to persecuting us. Jesus knew this would be the case for His disciples in His time and His disciples today. That's why He wrapped up His Beatitudes with Matthew 5:10-11.

Open your Bible and read Matthew 5:10-11. Then summarize this passage in your own words.

> Blessed are those who are persecuted because of righteousness, for theirs is the kingdom of heaven. Blessed are you when people insult you, persecute you and falsely say all kinds of evil against you because of me. — Matthew 5:10-11

Go to www.blueletterbible.com to find out what the key words mean. Record your findings in your journal.

If you found what I did, you could easily write, "Eternally happy and fortunate are those who have to run from others who try to stop them from living out God's righteous call on their lives; they will be elevated to a place of royalty and will be abundantly rewarded for all eternity."

As the story of Jonathan and David progresses in 1 Samuel 20, we learn that when King Saul (Jonathan's father) tried to have David killed, Jonathan warned David about it. David had done nothing wrong. He had lived a life above reproach, but Saul was so jealous that he couldn't see straight. Jonathan not only voiced his commitment to David, but he also proved his commitment. Jonathan made a plan with David: Jonathan would speak to his father about his intentions for David. Then Jonathan would go outside to shoot his bow and arrow. Based on what Saul told Jonathan, if Jonathan sent a young boy to fetch the arrows and come back to him, David was safe. But if the boy was sent out even farther, David would know that his life was in danger and that he needed to flee. After Jonathan spoke with his father, he went outside, shot the arrows, and sent the boy farther and farther out to get the arrows. Jonathan had proved his commitment to David. Though they both grieved that David would have to flee for his life, at least Jonathan had kept David safe from his father, who was out to destroy David. As they parted ways, they wept together and made the promise to always show kindness to the other's family (a promise David later kept).

Wrapping It Up

The best thing you can do for an intimate friend is protect her from those who would discourage her from fulfilling the purposes for which she was created. When someone persecutes you and discourages you from God's plans for you, you must flee from her and trust that God will protect you and reward you abundantly for your faithful commitment to His call on your life.

Apply It!

Seek Upwardly

Write the first line of 1 Corinthians 13:7 in your journal: "It [love] always protects." Draw an umbrella beside that verse and thank God for His never-ending protective love for you. The next time you carry an umbrella with you, remember that God loves you and is always protecting you, just like an umbrella protects you from the rain.

Seek Inwardly

Dialogue with God about what you learned today: Am I a discourager or an encourager? Are there people in my life who discourage me and from whom I need to distance myself? Ask God to open your eyes to those who may be discouraging you from becoming all He wants you to be.

Seek Outwardly

Ask God to help you know how to cheer on your friend to fulfill God's calling in her life. Ask Him to reveal those who are not supportive of her success and to give you wisdom about how to protect her from and warn her about that negativity.

Day 4: No Room for Takers

Pray, *Holy Spirit, be my Teacher. Give me understanding on how to put what I learn today into practice. In the name of Jesus I ask, amen.*

· · · · · · · · ·

At this level of friendship, there is no room for a one-sided relationship. The relationship must be reciprocated on both sides. With intimate friends, you are "all-in"—voicing commitment that is proven in your actions. This isn't all about one person fulfilling her purposes in life while the other does not. This is not about your friend supporting you without you supporting her. Instead, a mutual commitment to see both of you fulfill the purposes for which you were created drives your relationship.

When I started in ministry, a seasoned ministry leader named Jennifer Kennedy Dean (see her books on prayer) gave me one piece of advice: "Always promote others and let God promote you." I have carried that with me for all these years and it has proven true.

So often selfishness can get in the way and we can take advantage of our friend's loyal support. We can get so caught up in our own pursuit of possibilities that we forget to help others in the pursuit of theirs.

Many of us were raised with The Golden Rule. Do you remember it? Write it in your journal.

You probably wrote something like this: "Do unto others as you would have them do unto you." As I mentioned in week 5, this actually comes from the Bible. Jesus said it in Matthew 7:12. He was challenging His disciples to treat people the way they would want to be treated. What it does *not* say is, "Wait for someone to do something for you and then respond similarly." This is where we miss the total concept of reciprocated friendship because we limit it to reciprocating only *after* someone does something for us first! If that is the best way for us to relate to each other, we would all be sitting around waiting! Reciprocal friendships are mutual, with both giving to the relationship. When Jesus gave us this command, He said, "Do . . ." This is an imperative, which means Jesus was saying, "You! Do unto others as you would have them do unto you." So who does reciprocal friendship always start with? You!

> So in everything, do to others what you would have them do to you, for this sums up the Law and the Prophets. — Matthew 7:12

I know God has called me to be a student and proclaimer of His Word to help people walk with God and experience the abundant life He planned for them. The most loving thing others can do for me is to encourage me. So what would I want my friends to do for me as I write and travel to speak? I would want them to tell me when I do a good job. I would want them to help me get away so I can write. I would want them to tell me what is good about my writing and encourage me in areas that need some more work. I would want them to help me get my house cleaned, clothes washed and ready, and food bought for my family in my absence. Those actions would be a dream come true for me! They may be a little lofty but, hey, I can dream!

As you and your friend are discovering God's purposes for creating you and seeking to live those out, an intimate friend will picture what you could do and then will seek out God's help in planning ways to help you achieve your goals. This instills in you a sense of calling, a confidence in that friend's support, and a belief in you that you really can become all God wants you to be. It is a wonderful gift.

I had a major car wreck the summer before my senior year in high school. My mother met me at the emergency room, and she made this statement: "God left you on this earth for a purpose; you best find out what it is and do it with all your heart." Those are words that have never left me. They instilled in me a sense of calling, a sense of destiny. All of us need this encouragement from our friends.

Now here is the challenge: If I would want my friends to

challenge and encourage me and call out my giftedness, am I willing to do the same for them? Or am I too consumed with my own busyness that I have no room in my schedule to help out a friend? "Do unto others as you would have them do to you." You may need to evaluate if your expectations of others are realistic. You may also need to evaluate whether your commitment to others is lacking.

Wrapping It Up

If you want to fulfill God's purposes for you and you want the same for your intimate friends, you must be a giver, not always a taker. You must be willing to spur them on toward growth as you would want them to urge you on toward living out God's purposes for you.

Apply It!

Seek Upwardly

Write out The Golden Rule (Matthew 7:12) in your journal. Thank Him for all He gives and does for you. Confess, repent, and seek to offer your life as the least you can do for all He has done for you.

Seek Inwardly

Think about what you feel led to do and what you might want others to do to help you. Then treat your friends in the same way.

Seek Outwardly

Take some time to seek the Lord about a close friend and her purposes for being created. Ask the Father to help you encourage her, design projects for her, and invest in her so that she can be all He wants her to be, instilling in her a sense of purpose and destiny.

Day 5: A Promise to Be Made

Pray, *Holy Spirit, be my Teacher. Give me understanding on how to put what I learn today into practice. In the name of Jesus I ask, amen.*

. . . .

While writing this experiential guide, I have been refinishing a piece of furniture for my home. First I had to pick out the furniture that would best fit in my home. I tested it out in various places until I knew it was just the right piece. Then I began the process of stripping away all the old paint that had covered it over the years. As I stripped the wood, I uncovered layers of paint that I could not see from the surface. Once I got down to the original wood, I could see some flaws that needed to be repaired before I could finish my piece. Finally, I envisioned just how I wanted my piece to look when it was complete, and I began working toward that end. I am still putting the finishing touches on the piece, and while it has been a work in progress, I am so proud of what this once old, now new piece of furniture has become. It will soon adorn my home because I was committed to finishing this piece, taking it through every phase of its "becoming."

Above all that we have learned throughout this study, the greatest truth is this: In order for friendships to grow, they require commitment for the long haul. Throughout the guide, we have correlated friendship to a puzzle. We usually don't stop putting a puzzle together until it is complete. What an awesome thought that not only is God faithful to finish what He started in you, but He also allows you to be a part of seeing that happen for someone else. May I suggest we all make this commitment to our intimate friends as we seek to discover and then live out The Possibilities God has for us?

"I will proclaim my commitment to my friends in both word and deed."

This means that I will say you are my friend and also prove it by the way I live.

Just as we have learned in previous weeks, God has certainly made this same commitment to you: **"I have and will continue to proclaim My commitment to you in both word and deed."**

He told us and showed us His love through His death, resurrection, and deposit of His Spirit within us. What a Savior! What a Friend!

Now here comes a hard question to ponder: If we don't want our friends to just say that they are our friends but also to prove their commitment to us by their actions, isn't it reasonable for God to desire the same from us? Are you willing to make a fresh commitment to God and say, **"I will proclaim my commitment to You in both word and deed"?**

James 1:22 put it like this: "Do not merely listen to the word, and so deceive yourselves. Do what it says."

Do you remember the promise that David and Jonathan made prior to David fleeing from the hand of King Saul? They promised to be kind to each other's families as long as they lived. But Jonathan added an interesting phrase: "even when the LORD has cut off every one of David's enemies from the face of the earth" (1 Samuel 20:15). It was as if Jonathan knew David well enough to know that while David might remember to show kindness to Jonathan's family in the heat of the battles (when they were right in his face), he might forget to care for them when things had died down and David was at peace.

At the close of 1 Samuel and the opening of 2 Samuel, both King Saul and Jonathan were killed in battle. Finally King David was at peace, defeating every enemy who threatened him. Then, long after Jonathan's death, look at what the Scripture says about the promise he had made.

Open your Bible and read 2 Samuel 9:1-11. Consider what you might do given the same situation.

David asked, "Is there anyone still left of the house of Saul to whom I can show kindness for Jonathan's sake?"

Now there was a servant of Saul's household named Ziba. They called him to appear before David, and the king said to him, "Are you Ziba?"

"Your servant," he replied.

The king asked, "Is there no one still left of the house of Saul to whom I can show God's kindness?"

Ziba answered the king, "There is still a son of Jonathan; he is crippled in both feet."

"Where is he?" the king asked.

Ziba answered, "He is at the house of Makir son of Ammiel in Lo Debar."

So King David had him brought from Lo Debar, from the house of Makir son of Ammiel.

When Mephibosheth son of Jonathan, the son of Saul, came to David, he bowed down to pay him honor.

David said, "Mephibosheth!"

"Your servant," he replied.

"Don't be afraid," David said to him, "for I will surely show you kindness for the sake of your father Jonathan. I will restore to you all the land that belonged to your grandfather Saul, and you will always eat at my table."

Mephibosheth bowed down and said, "What is your servant, that you should notice a dead dog like me?"

Then the king summoned Ziba, Saul's servant, and said to him, "I have given your master's grandson everything that belonged to Saul and his family. You and your sons and your servants are to farm the land for him and bring in the crops, so that your master's grandson may be provided for. And Mephibosheth, grandson of your master, will always eat at my table." (Now Ziba had fifteen sons and twenty servants.)

> Then Ziba said to the king, "Your servant will do whatever my lord the king commands his servant to do." So Mephibosheth ate at David's table like one of the king's sons. — 2 Samuel 9:1-11

Though Jonathan was no longer alive to hold him to his commitment, King David remained loyal and kept his promise to show kindness to Jonathan's family. This is the essence of true intimate friendship—loyalty and commitment expressed in a verbal promise and backed by faithful action. That is what we long for in our intimate friendships, and that is what our Father longs for in our relationship with Him.

Wrapping It Up

As you come to the end of your study on living in relationships, feel a sense of satisfaction that you completed this with God. Ask the Holy Spirit to help you put into practice all that you have learned through your time with Him; ask in the name of Jesus.

Apply It!

Seek Upwardly

Write this friendship commitment in your journal and refer to it throughout your day and the days to come. Write out James 1:22 and offer God your commitment to not just proclaim that you are a Christian but to obey His words and prove it by your actions.

Seek Inwardly

Ask God to help you support your friends in word and actions, helping them succeed in all that God wants to make of their lives. And as this study on friendships comes to an end, ask God to seal His truth in your heart and mind so that you can live it out for the rest of your days.

Seek Outwardly

Begin to back up your words with actions that build in your friends a confidence to explore the possibilities that lie before them. Learn to help friends flee the naysayers who seek to discourage them. Outserve each other in reciprocated friendship so that both of you become who God meant for you to be.

Looking Back

At the beginning of this study, you were asked to draw a picture that represented what your current relationships look like. Then you were asked to draw a picture of what you want them to look like as you begin to apply what you have learned in this study. Pull those pictures out again and reflect on what you have learned, how your perspective has changed, and how your actions have changed as a result. Note how far you've come in your time with God and thank Him for all He has taught you.

Thank you for joining me for the *Connect* study! If you would like to stay connnected with me as you continue your path of discipleship, I would love to hear from you about how this study affected your life. Simply go to www.livingdeeperministries.com and join a host of other women who want to be disciples of Jesus and take others with them. You will find great encouragement for your journey there.

Surrendered,
Jena

how to become
a Christian

This section may be the most important one you read in this entire book. Everything else that is written will not compare to what God will do through your life as you surrender to Him. No life will ever reach the heights intended unless one is born again. Read what is written, talk to God, and follow Him by accepting Jesus as your Lord. After you decide to follow Jesus, you will never be the same again. May God transform you into the person He desires you to be as you allow Jesus to become the Savior of your soul and the Lord of your life.

Recognize That God Loves You

> For God so loved the world that he gave his one and only Son, that whoever believes in him shall not perish but have eternal life. (John 3:16)

Recognize That You Have Sinned

> For all have sinned and fall short of the glory of God. (Romans 3:23)

Recognize That Sin's Debt Must Be Paid

For the wages of sin is death, but the gift of God is eternal life in Christ Jesus our Lord. (Romans 6:23)

Recognize That Christ Paid for Your Sins

But God demonstrates his own love for us in this: While we were still sinners, Christ died for us. (Romans 5:8)

Pray and Receive Christ Today

Everyone who calls on the name of the Lord will be saved. (Romans 10:13)

For he says, "In the time of my favor I heard you, and in the day of salvation I helped you." I tell you, now is the time of God's favor, now is the day of salvation. (2 Corinthians 6:2)

Today you can receive Jesus as your Lord and Savior.

If you agree with the Scriptures you just read, simply pray this prayer aloud:

Dear Jesus, I invite You to forgive me of my sins and come into my heart and life right now. I receive Your gift of payment for my sins by dying in my place.

I accept You, Jesus, as my Lord and Savior. Please reveal Yourself to me and become real in my life from this moment forward. Thank You for saving me and giving me eternal life. I love You and commit my life to You. Amen.

What to Do Now?

I want to encourage you to do the following three things as a response
to your decision:

1. Tell someone. Tell a close friend, your spouse, and even tell
   me! I would love to hear from you about your decision to
   follow Jesus! E-mail me at jena@livingdeeperministries.com
   and let me know.
2. Find a church home that will baptize you and nurture you in
   your new walk with the Lord.
3. Commit to grow daily in your new Christian life by reading
   the Bible, praying, and having fellowship with other believers.

about the author

JENA FOREHAND experienced firsthand God's power to transform a life when He healed her broken marriage in 1997. With a spirit of authenticity, Jena and her husband, Dale, began ministering to other couples through marriage conferences, retreats, and resources. She was next drawn to women's ministry and the incredible need for living in deeper relationship with God through discipleship.

Jena's passion for Christ is evident as she writes and speaks clearly, comically, and candidly to women. When not traveling with her husband and family, she focuses her time and energy on how to best partner with future generations in discipleship. Jena lives in Birmingham, Alabama, with her family.

The essential guide to mentoring millennials, woman to woman

Living Deeper
Jena Forehand

Launch an exciting, impactful ministry to the millennial generation through a whole new vision of discipleship. *Living Deeper* is a foundational guide that provides everything needed to lead young women into a deeper relationship with Christ. Candid truth about the perspective of millennials offers vital insights into a generation whose view of church and faith differs from any before. Meaningful questions and helpful tips prepare you to disciple others. With a warm, often lighthearted tone, it's the perfect guide to helping young women, whether new in Christ or spiritually searching, find a faith that transforms.

978-1-61291-428-2

To order copies, call NavPress at **1-800-366-7788** or log on to **www.NavPress.com**.

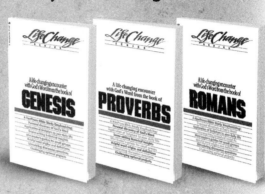

The Message Means Understanding

Bringing the Bible to all ages

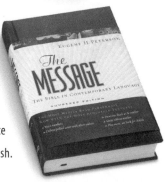

*T*he *Message* is written in
contemporary language that is
much like talking with a good friend.
When paired with your favorite Bible study,
The Message will deliver a reading experience
that is reliable, energetic, and amazingly fresh.

N A V E S S E N T I A L S

Voices of The Navigators—Past, Present, and Future

WANT MORE
JERRY BRIDGES STUDIES?

CHALLENGE YOUR SMALL GROUP WITH THESE ALL-IN-ONE CURRICULUM SETS FROM BEST-SELLING AUTHOR JERRY BRIDGES!

Each curriculum set includes the book in its entirety as well as a discussion guide.

∧ Respectable Sins Small-Group Curriculum

Jerry Bridges addresses the issue that no sin is tolerable in God's eyes.

Nine-week study | 9781615215775

∧ Transforming Grace Small-Group Curriculum

Experience true freedom from a performance-driven world with God's daily transforming grace.

Eight-week study | 9781615215713

∧ The Practice of Godliness Small-Group Curriculum

Grow in Christian character and learn how to establish the foundation upon which that character is built.

Twelve-week study | 9781615215836

∧ The Pursuit of Holiness Small-Group Curriculum

What is holiness, and how do we pursue it?

Twelve-week study | 9781615215843

To order copies, call NavPress at **1-800-366-7788** or log on to **www.NavPress.com**.

NAVPRESS

Discipleship Inside Out™